1,000,000 Books

are available to read at

Forgotten Books

www.ForgottenBooks.com

Read online
Download PDF
Purchase in print

ISBN 978-1-331-31436-3
PIBN 10173089

1 MONTH OF
FREE
READING

at

www.ForgottenBooks.com

By purchasing this book you are eligible for one month membership to ForgottenBooks.com, giving you unlimited access to our entire collection of over 1,000,000 titles via our web site and mobile apps.

To claim your free month visit:

www.forgottenbooks.com/free173089

English
Français
Deutsche
Italiano
Español
Português

www.forgottenbooks.com

Mythology Photography **Fiction**
Fishing Christianity **Art** Cooking
Essays Buddhism Freemasonry
Medicine **Biology** Music **Ancient**
Egypt Evolution Carpentry Physics
Dance Geology **Mathematics** Fitness
Shakespeare **Folklore** Yoga Marketing
Confidence Immortality Biographies
Poetry **Psychology** Witchcraft
Electronics Chemistry History **Law**
Accounting **Philosophy** Anthropology
Alchemy Drama Quantum Mechanics
Atheism Sexual Health **Ancient History**
Entrepreneurship Languages Sport
Paleontology Needlework Islam
Metaphysics Investment Archaeology
Parenting Statistics Criminology
Motivational

A VISIT

TO

MY FATHER-LAND,

BEING NOTES OF A JOURNEY TO SYRIA AND
PALESTINE IN 1843.

"If I forget thee, O Jerusalem, let my right hand forget her
cunning."—Ps. cxxxvii. 6.

BY

RIDLEY H. HERSCHELL,

AUTHOR OF A "BRIEF SKETCH OF THE JEWS," &c. &c.

Fifth Thousand.

LONDON:

J. UNWIN, 31, BUCKLERSBURY,

W. S. KENNEDY, EDINBURGH; J. MACLEHOSE, GLASGOW.

1845.

LONDON:
J. UNWIN, PRINTER, 31, BUCKLERSBURY.

TO

SIR CULLING EARDLEY SMITH, BART.

My Beloved Friend,

It may appear absurd to dedicate this humble production to any one; but I feel pleasure in thus acknowledging my gratitude to you, by whose kindness my visit to my father-land was planned, and through whose liberality it was accomplished.

This visit has been productive of much enjoyment to me, in which enjoyment you would have largely participated, had you been able, as at first proposed, to visit Palestine along with me; since, so far from being ashamed to claim affinity with the despised Jew, I know it is rather a source of gratification to you that you are connected with the seed of Abraham. And however the expression of my feelings in regard to the Eastern churches may be viewed by others, I know you will join me in regretting, that any British Christians should have thrown an additional stumbling-block in the way of the Jews, by recognising these corrupt communions as churches of Christ.

I am, my beloved Friend,

Gratefully and affectionately yours,

RIDLEY H. HERSCHELL.

London May, 1st, 1844.

PREFACE

I cannot allow another edition of this little work to go forth, without expressing my thankfulness, that, with all its faults, it has been so favourably received by the public. I am well aware that some things I have said in it are very unpalateable to many whom I sincerely love. I have been asked to purge it of these, and to reduce it to a simple statement regarding the present appearance of those localities mentioned in Scripture. To this I can only reply: God forbid that I should ever cease to testify against that which I believe He sees to be evil. If what I have said were not in some measure felt to be *true,* it would not have caused the annoyance it has done to some sincere Christians. These are not times for temporising : " Let God be true, and every man a liar," in so far as he opposes the truth of God.

I have been told that some, who cannot impugn the truth of any thing I have stated, have imputed unworthy motives to me in making the statements I have done. With this I have nothing to do ; they, and not I, must answer for their evil surmises. It would be absurd to expect our course to be as smooth and pleasant when we go against the general current of religious opinion, as it is when we glide along with it.

It has gratified me much to learn that this humble publication has been the means of drawing the attention of many to the study of the prophetic scriptures. May it continue to be thus honored.

London, October 1st, 1845.

CONTENTS.

A VISIT

MY FATHER-LAND.

THERE are already so many journals of travels
in Palestine, as well as more elaborate and
valuable works illustrative of scripture history
and customs, that I at first determined to
confine myself to a few observations on the
state of my brethren, the Jews, unconnected
with any personal narrative, or notice of the
country of my fathers.   But when I consider
that all these works are beyond the reach of
the poor of Christ's flock, and that many of
the middle class, also, have not leisure to peruse
them, I feel it right, for their sakes, to mention
something about those places that are interesting to every one who loves the word of God.
This I have chosen to dö in the mode which I
knew would be most agreeable to those who

B

have the first claim on me, the people under my pastoral care, by giving the substance of the journal written at each place ; as, to them at least, the impression made, and the thoughts suggested, on the spot, will be far more interesting than any more elaborate description drawn up afterwards. For the same reason, I shall not confine my observations to Palestine, but make such remarks as occurred to me on the moral and religious state of the different countries through which I passed on my way thither. The present state of the professing Church of Christ is not only interesting to all who have the glory of God at heart, but is intimately connected with the subject which at present occupies so many minds, the conversion of my brethren, the Jews, to Christianity.

Besides the above, I feel that I have another, and a less pleasing duty to perform. A conflict has arisen in these latter days between the word of God and the word of man, in a quarter where such a conflict was supposed long since to have terminated. If "teaching for doctrine the commandments of men," be attended with evil, even amid the Protestant light of England, how disastrous must be its consequences amid the darkness of Greek and Romish superstition! Yet many of the saints of God, who see and mourn over its evil developments in British colonies and foreign countries, are, from their peculiar position, hampered in their testimony against them. Against these I feel that I must testify boldly. This is no time to wink at evil, and speak smoothly of it, in order to please men. A matter that in itself is merely trifling and absurd, may become a soul-destroying error, if it countenance and confirm men in their allegiance to those corrupt communities, falsely called Christian churches, that degrade the religion of Christ into a routine of outward forms and observances. I believe we have arrived at the time when every thing that can be shaken, must and shall be shaken, that the things which cannot be shaken, and they only, may remain.* Let not the Lord's people seek to prop up any thing that is false. "How does God view this? Does the idea, conveyed to the

---

* Heb. xii. 26, 27.

minds of men by this or that practice or form of words, accord with His eternal truth?" This is the test to which we must bring all things: these questions, solemnly put, as in His sight, would at once solve many difficulties, and prevent all resort to that modern loophole, the *non-natural* sense. The events that are daily passing around us, loudly call on us to oppose the spirit of Antichrist, whether it meet us in the form of professed Protestantism, or of Greek or Romish superstition.

The details of my intercourse with the Jews would give additional interest to the journal, if introduced in their proper places; but this I have resolved to avoid; and to give what relates to them in a separate form at the end. Nothing can be more hurtful to the cause of Christianity among them, than the reporting of conversations held with them upon the subject, with such circumstances of time and place being mentioned, as point them out to their townsmen or acquaintances. If a respectable Jew find that he cannot converse on Christianity with a missionary, or a converted brother, without its being blazoned abroad, he will naturally be reluctant to do so; and the intercourse between English and foreign Jews is so constant, that whatever is published concerning them in this country, soon becomes known on the continent.

Having made these few preliminary remarks, I shall now proceed to give such extracts from my journal, as I think will be acceptable to the class for whom it is chiefly intended; adding such reflections as occurred to me either at the time or afterwards. In supplying such information as may be necessary for readers who have not perused other works on the subject, I shall freely make use of the descriptions and statements of abler writers than myself.

I left home, accompanied by my friend, Mr. J. F. M., on the 9th of February, 1843, and reached Paris on the 11th. Although in London we are too well used to the sight of vanity and sin, yet there is something in the ungodliness of Paris that cannot fail to strike one on entering it for the first time, or on returning to it after a long absence. You

seem to behold the awful sight of a city
wholly given over to the service of sin and
folly. But it is a comfort to know that even
here, there are a few of the children of God.
It was delightful, in the midst of all this evil,
to unite with a little flock of true worshippers;
who have been called out of the errors of
Popery, and the darkness of nature, into the
marvellous light of the Gospel. The Rev.
Mark Wilks has done, and is doing, a great
work in Paris; and it is very desirable that his
schools, and other schemes of usefulness,
should receive more aid from the Christian
people of Britain than they have yet enjoyed.
The salvation of souls should be equally
precious in their sight, whether this is sought
to be accomplished on the plains of Africa, or
in the lanes of Paris.

At Lyons, also, there is an interesting work
going on, similar to that in Paris. The labours
of the Rev. C. A. Cordes, the French Protestant
pastor, have been greatly blessed; and the
schools here, as well as in Paris, have been
of much use, not only to Gentile, but also
to some Jewish children. One little anecdote

I must mention. Mrs. Cordes was one day questioning the girls on religious subjects, and asked one little girl what was the ground of her hope for eternity. The child answered: " That Christ died for me." On hearing this reply, a number of the children cried out: "Oh! she is a Jewess, and yet she says Christ died for her!" " Well," rejoined the little girl, "though I am a Jewess, still Christ died for me." How remarkable it is, that, even in childhood, the Gentiles are accustomed to look on the Jews as strangers and outcasts!

At Avignon I was much interested by the ruins of the Pope's palace, the scene of the martyrdom of many of the saints of God. We were shown first into the chapel, where was the altar before which the children of God, bound with chains, had to make a declaration of their faith. We were then shown the dungeon where they had been imprisoned; upon the walls of which are still legible several texts of scripture inscribed by these faithful witnesses for the truth.—" Blessed are they that hunger and thirst after righteousness, for they shall be filled:" "Watch and pray that ye enter not into temptation:" "He shall call upon me, and I will answer him. I will be with him in trouble; I will deliver him, and honour him." These, and many other appropriate texts, are still to be seen. These saints, who "loved not their lives unto the death," being dead, yet speak; telling us to be faithful and uncompromising; to resist, if need be, even "unto blood, striving against sin," and false religion. They also testify how precious, to the suffering saint, is the revealed word of God; and how, in all circumstances, the same blessed truths are the staff and stay of God's people.

We were also shown a curiously-constructed place, strong and massively built, something like a brick-kiln, with a sort of chimney at the top. Here some precious sons and daughters of God were burned to death "for the testimony of Jesus;" part of the wall is still discoloured by the smoke of the fagots. After this we were conducted to the torture room, in which some of the instruments of

torture still remain ;—awful tokens of that
persecuting church, which hates the light now
as much as ever it did.

At Nice and Genoa I enjoyed much delightful intercourse with English Christians ; but
nothing can be more melancholy than the
religious state of Italy. I have seen much of
Popery both in Prussia and France ; but in
neither of these countries has it been able to
" take away the key of knowledge ;" refusing
to enter in, and hindering those who would.
But in Italy this is done most effectually. In
the Sardinian dominions, not a Bible, nor a
religious tract, can be given away without the
risk of imprisonment. About two years
since, a Swiss gentleman went to the baths
at Aix, in Savoy. A woman was employed as
a spy, who professed to be a Protestant, and
asked him for some religious books. He
complied with her request ; she took them
immediately to the priest, and the priest to the
police ; and in a few hours after he gave the
books, he was thrown into a dungeon with
the lowest criminals, where he was kept for
nine months. A similar attempt was made

to entrap a friend of mine, when he was staying at Oneglia. The police tried to persuade the waiter of the inn to ask the loan of books from him; and induced an old Italian gentleman in the town to ask Bibles with the same view. Happily my friend was aware of their devices, and escaped the snare.

On the 18th of March I arrived in Rome. I might fill a volume with the reflections which this wonderful city naturally suggests; but my limits forbid more than a few brief notices. Among the numerous remains of heathen magnificence, cruelty, and super-stition, one of those which most powerfully affected me, was the arch of Titus. This was raised to commemorate the conquest of Jerusalem by that emperor. A train of captive Jews, together with the table, the seven-branched candlestick, and the vessels of the temple, are sculptured upon it. What a monument of the faithfulness of God's judgments! "Because thou servedst not the Lord thy God,—the Lord shall bring a nation against thee from far, from the end of the earth, as swift as the eagle flieth;—and ye shall be plucked from off the land whither thou goest to possess it."*

But if this ancient memorial of the captivity of my people affected me, how much more did the sight of their present captivity in this which calls itself the "holy city!" I have witnessed their oppression and degradation in many parts of the continent; but never did I see them so "trodden down" as in Rome. They live in a certain part of the city called the Ghetto, closed in by two gates, at each of which stands a sentinel; and so strictly are they confined to this place, that, when the Tiber overflowed many of their houses, a short time since, the sufferers were not allowed to move out of it, to obtain even temporary accommodation in another quarter. Close to one of the gates is a church, on the outside of which is a representation of the crucifixion, under which there is written, in Hebrew, "I have spread out my hands all the day unto a rebellious people."† No Jew can go out

* Deut. xxviii. 47, 49, 63.   † Isa. lxv. 2.

or in by this gate without beholding what he can only regard as a studied insult to his feelings. Did the Pope and his cardinals ever read the Epistle to the Romans, given forth by the Holy Ghost through Paul? "Boast not against the branches,—thou bearest not the root, but the root thee." How wonder·fully has professing Christendom overlooked God's oft-repeated declaration, that, though He punishes the Jews for their iniquity, He is "sore displeased" with others who "help on the affliction!"

I went to St. Peter's on the day the Pope, during Lent, pays a weekly visit to it. What a sight this was! In England we have much of the spirit of Popery; but of what may be called its *material* part, its outward embody-ment, we know nothing. Hence it is, that those who denounce Popery as idolatry, are often regarded as bigoted fanatics, or, at least, as persons, who, in their zeal for Protestantism, are guilty of gross exaggeration. But for any one who has been in Rome to speak in measured terms of Popery, is a melancholy illustration how the love of system and of party can bring a man deliberately to " call evil good, and good evil."

St. Peter's is a splendid edifice, and the Pope was attended by a retinue quite in keeping with it ; Swiss guards, officers in rich uniforms, cardinals in their red robes, courtiers in state dresses, " gold, and silver, and fine linen, and purple, and silk, and scarlet," " the lust of the eye, and the pride of life," every thing that is " of the world," and is " not of the Father," accompanied this representative of the poor fisherman of Bethsaida. The professed object of his visit to St. Peter's was to worship the invisible God, " whom no man hath seen nor can see." And what was his first act ? He knelt down to a bronze statue, originally made to represent Jupiter, but now called St. Peter ; he put his head under the foot of this statue, remaining in this attitude for two minutes ; then put his lips on the foot for about as long. If this were not worshipping Peter, I know not what outward worship means. And what is the natural effect of this on the mind of the gnorant ? To carry them one degree lower in the scale of idolatry, even to the worship of the piece of senseless bronze before them. I saw a mother take her little infant, and rub its face on the toe of the image. Many of the ignorant populace of Popish countries are as complete worshippers of wood and stone, as the heathen inhabitants of the South Sea Islands. That they have profaned the holy name of Jesus by bestowing it on one of their idols; and have been made acquainted with a confused jumble of broken fragments of Scripture history and doctrine, certainly cannot entitle them to the name of Christians.

That the Virgin Mary is worshipped as a goddess is well known, and has been often stated and proved; but among their "lords many, and gods many," I became acquainted in Rome with one of whom I had never before heard. I one day observed the waiter at the restaurateur's where I dined reading a little book with seriousness and attention. I asked what it was; he told me it was a book of prayers. Suspecting it to be prayers to the Virgin, I asked to whom the prayers were addressed. "To Saint Anna." I enquired who Saint Anna was; and was told she was the "grandmother of God!" This book of prayers I purchased of him, and will now give some account of, that the religion of modern Rome may be fairly estimated.

It is a small pamphlet of twenty-four pages, printed at Rome in 1830. The title is, '' Devout Exercises in honour of the most glorious mother Saint Anna; which are prae-tised every Tuesday in the year, in the parish church of St. John the Evangelist, by a pious assembly of devotees of the said Anna." The origin of this pious assembly is first set forth; and is said to be, "That seeing there is but a small attendance of the faithful at the church of St. John, on occasion of the holy viaticum being carried to the sick, some devout persons (concurrently with the orders and wishes of Pope Clement XIII., published on the 22nd December, 1758, by Cardinal Guadagni, then vicar of his holiness) thought of establishing, in this venerable church, a pious assembly, or confraternity of brothers and sisters, under the auspices of the most holy sacrament, and of the glorious mother, Saint Anna, whom they

chose as their special protectress." A copy of
the decree of the vicar-general, testifying the
Pope's approbation of this pious union, is next
given. Then follow several prayers to Saint
Anna, and a summary of the indulgences
granted to this faithful company of brothers
and sisters.

The prayers bid defiance to the Jesuitical
distinctions between the two kinds of worship,
latria, and *dulia* ; the one kind paid to God,
and the other to the saints. I can afford space
for but few extracts ; but these few will fully
bear out this assertion.

"We congratulate you, O glorious Saint
Anna, who, for your eminent virtues and
sublime sanctity, were chosen by God to be
the mother of the queen of angels ; and, pros-
trate at your feet, we pray you with all our
heart to obtain for us, from the divine incar-
nate word, the pardon of our sins. "We
supplicate you to obtain from God for us, that
our prayers may be favourably heard."

The same sentiments are repeated in different words in every prayer ; and in several of
them there is no mention made of our blessed

Saviour. Why should there be; these Romish
idolaters have other Saviours, and other inter-
cessors. In proof of this I transcribe the
whole of the third prayer.*

"We adore you, O glorious Saint Anna;
and by that unspeakable joy which you experienced, when the most holy soul of Mary
was united in your bosom to her most pure
body, we humbly pray you to obtain for us
from God, by your most efficacious intercession,
that we may be pure in mind and body, in
order to enjoy His presence, promised to those
who are clean of heart. Amen."

This absurd and impious idolatry reaches its
climax in the following prayer (which I also
give entire), in which there is no mention of
God at all; the two goddesses, Anna and
Mary, being able of themselves to bestow
divine grace and protection.

"We bless you through all ages, O glorious
Saint Anna; and by the joy which your heart
felt in touching, caressing, and imprinting

* I do not feel it necessary to give the original
Italian, as it is probable the whole book will be re-
printed, with a translation.

kisses, not less pure than tender, on the most
pure face of the babe Mary, your daughter, we
humbly pray you to implore from the same,
our lady, her most efficacious protection and
grace, that we be not deceived by the cunning
of the infernal enemy, and may avoid every
criminal act, however small.   Amen."

I shall conclude my notice of this extraordinary manual of devotion, by some
extracts from an act of self-dedication to
Saint Anna.

"O most glorious and most blessed Saint
Anna, mother of the great mother of God,
I. N., in presence of all the court of heaven,
elect and confirm you to be, after Jesus and
Mary, my chief advocate and mother; I
declare my desire always to esteem, serve,
and love you as such, all the term of my life.

"I am rejoiced at your high sanctity,
dignity, and glory, in your having for a
daughter the queen of heaven.

"I propose to exert all my power to promote your glory; and to do the utmost I can,
that you may be revered and loved.   Deign
to receive me into the number of your servants;

to adopt me for your son; and to keep me ever under the mantle of your protection.

" Procure me light, and inward grief for my sins; make me amend my life, and imitate those virtues, by which you were so pleasing to the divine eyes.

"Come, most compassionate mother, together with your most delightful daughter, to my aid and defence, when I shall be presented at the divine tribunal, to be judged for all the years and days of my life. Deliver me from that horrible sentence, and from the eternal pains of hell, that I have so many times deserved."

All comment on this would be superfluous; and this book, bearing on its title page the sanction of Papal authority, was given to this poor man by a priest! We can only cry, " O Lord, how long!" I cannot help saying, that I regard the tractarian heresy as a judgment on the church of England, for her sin in recognising the orders of the " man of sin," instead of protesting against Rome, as no church of Christ at all, but a system of idolatry.

But I must linger no longer in Rome; one

feature more of the " mystery of iniquity," and
I have done.

One day, in company with some friends, I
visited the mint. We were shown a cabinet
containing medals struck in the reigns of the
various Popes. The dies of these are all preserved ; and the government officers willingly
strike off as many of them as the visitors
please to purchase. One would imagine that
some few of them would have been prudently
left in the shade, or rather that the dies would
have been destroyed, so that no memorial of
the coins might remain. If medals had been
struck in England, in commemoration of the
atrocities of Mary's reign, or of the legal
murders of that of Charles the Second, they
would not have been preserved and struck off
in the present day, but would have been in-
dignantly disowned by succeeding governments.
Not so the unchangeable papacy ; it is no wise
ashamed of any of its previous acts ; but gives
you such coins as the following, with the same
readiness with which the English would present
a foreigner with a Waterloo medal.

The destroying angel, with a cross in one

hand and a spear in the other: Inscription, "Massacre of the Huguenots,"* 1575. Reverse, "Gregorius XIII. Pont. Max. An. I."

A wild boar hunt: Inscription, "The pious shepherd wages war only against wild beasts."† Reverse, "Paulus II. Venetus. Pont. Max.

Paul II. ascended the Papal throne in 1464, and fiercely persecuted the Lollards; the boar hunt, therefore, must refer to them, who were indeed hunted like wild beasts.

Christ driving the buyers and sellers out of the temple: Inscription, "My house shall be called a house of prayer."‡ Reverse, "Paulus IV. Pont. OP.T.M."

This no doubt refers to that pontiff's proposed expulsion of the Jews from Rome.

But perhaps the most surprising of the whole, is the following honest confession in hard metal, of what is so often denied in words; namely, that they worship the Pope.

Crowning the Pope: Inscription, "Whom

---

* Ugonottorum Strages.
† Solum in feras pius bellatur pastor.
‡ Domus mea domus orationis voc.

they create they adore."* Reverse, "Adrianus VI. Pont. Maxim."

This candid acknowledgment that, like the heathen, they worship the work of their own hands, is a degree of simplicity one hardly expected in Romanists.

On the 30th of March we left Rome by the diligence. It appeared very odd to see upon the coach, and upon the sleeves of the postilion's coat, the mitre and keys. This is rather an extraordinary practical commentary upon the verse, "Thou art Peter, and upon this rock I will build my church." The spiritual head of a kingdom, "not of this world," uses the keys of the kingdom of heaven as a mark of earthly sovereignty! In travelling through the Pope's dominions, one is constantly reminded of the unscriptural nature of his pretensions. Who can look on one of his soldiers, for example, without being reminded of the words, "My kingdom is not of this world; if my kingdom were of this world, then would my servants fight."†

---

* Quem creant adorant.   † John xviii. 36

I cannot say that the Pope's diligences are at all arranged for the comfort of the passengers ; nor can I speak very favourably of their speed. I often thought of the proverb that speaks of making mountains of mole-hills ; for at every little rise in the road, we had bullocks to help us up ; and at every little descent, the wheel was locked, and again was unlocked, by a little winding machine that made no small noise, which at night was a great disturbance and annoyance to us.

On the third day after leaving Rome, we arrived at Loretto. This place is famous for one of the lying wonders of Popery. It is said that the angels lifted up the house of the Virgin Mary in Nazareth, and flew with it to Loretto, where it now stands in the inside of a church. Soon after our arrival we went to visit this church. It is much resorted to by pilgrims from all quarters, who go there to worship "the mother of God," as they blasphemously call her. The interior of the church is rather handsome ; but the great object of attraction is a small square building within it, called the

Virgin's house.   The outside of it is decorated
with sculptured figures of the prophets, and a
white marble pavement; which latter is much
worn by the poor deluded worshippers, whose
practice is to go round it on their knees.   On
entering the door, which is guarded by a soldier,
you get into a small apartment, from which the
light of heaven is excluded, and a few lamps
shed a dim light around, a fit emblem of this
false religion.   In this stands a figure of the
Virgin, as large as life, dressed up, and
ornamented with sparkling jewels; and the
lamps are so arranged as to throw a bright
light upon this figure, while every other object
is in shade.   We were much struck with the
resemblance of this image to that of Diana of
Ephesus, which we had seen at the Capitol.
On seeing this idol, I could not help asking
myself, "Am I in Europe, and in the nine-
teenth century?"   Yes, in this enlightened
age, thousands of devotees come to pay their
homage to this dressed doll; and yet Italy is
called by courtesy a *Christian* country!   Is it
reasonable to expect that any one who is con-

cerned for the honour of his Lord, can speak
in measured terms of such a system of lies as
Popery ?

We reached Ancona on the 1st of April, and
on the evening of the second we embarked on
board of an Austrian steamer. One of our
fellow-passengers was a Jew ; and as an interview on the high seas is not liable to the
objections that attend reporting an interview
on land, I may mention that I had much
interesting conversation with him. He seemed
an upright and sincere man, and entered
readily into conversation with me. One evening after the other passengers had retired, he
came to me and said, that his mind had been
very much disturbed and unsettled about the
coming of the Messiah. He had always been
taught to believe that before His coming, the
Jews were to become more religious ; but instead of this, they are becoming more and more
ungodly, and if this be so, will the Messiah ever
come ?   I told him, that to me, who believe He
has already come, as the one great sacrifice for
sin, this is no difficulty ; as He himself says in
reference to His second coming, " When the

Son of Man cometh, shall he find faith on the earth?" He said this to Jews, and it is literally taking place among them; but God is not leaving Himself without witnesses, as the prophet has said, "Except the Lord of Hosts had left unto us a very small remnant, we should have been as Sodom, and we should have been like unto Gomorrah."* This small remnant of witnesses consists of truly religious Jews, who believe in Jesus Christ as their Messiah, and walk in holiness of life. I then asked him what he meant by being religious? He said, putting on the phylacteries, by which we are reminded of God's commandments; and repeating about the sacrifices, which reminds us of God's pardoning mercy. I asked him what scriptural authority there was for putting on phylacteries? He seemed amazed at my ignorance, and repeated the passage in Deut. vi. 6, 8. "And these words which I command thee this day shall be in thine heart, and thou shall bind them for a sign upon thine hand, and they shall be as frontlets between thine

* Isaiah i. 9.

eyes." I told him that if God meant the
words of Moses to be put into a leather case,
it ought to be the whole books of Moses, and
not merely one passage from them; but that
any one giving heed to the spirit of that
chapter, and not to the mere letter, would
see it had a far deeper meaning than binding
on a few words of the law to the forehead and
arm; that it meant the laying up of God's
precepts in the heart, and practising them in
the life and conversation. He still insisted
that if it were not for the phylactery, and
other outward observances, there would be no
religion at all among the Jews; and that for
the sake of the unlearned, especially, it is
necessary to have many outward observances.
I reminded him that one of the blessings
promised at the coming of the Messiah, is,
that to the meek or poor the good tidings of
salvation is to be announced; and that, " the
wayfaring man, though a simple one, shall not
err" in the way of holiness. I then explained
to him how the pardoning love of God is
seen in Christ Jesus; and how I can behold
in Him, Jehovah tzidkenu, the Lord our

righteousness ; that I see in Him my re-
surrection from the dead, and look forward
with confidence to His second coming in glory,
when this corruptible shall put on incorruption,
and this mortal shall put on immortality.   He
said, " I wish I could believe all this ; but
business occupies my thoughts so much, that
I have no time for thinking on these things ;
and besides this, I live in a bigoted Roman
Catholic country, where all the displays of their
religious ceremonies are very offensive to the
feelings of a devout Jew ; and if I wished to
become a Christian, I must, by the law of the
land, become a Roman Catholic; and I have
seen so much wickedness and bigotry among
the Jews who become Romanists, that I shrink
from the idea of becoming one of them."   He
then related to me several cases of Jews who
have·become Jesuits, which I do not consider
myself at liberty to repeat.

On April 4th we cast anchor at Corfu ; and
we called immediately on Mr. Lowndes, of the
London Missionary Society, who received us
very kindly.   He showed us the different
schools established here by government, and

by the London Missionary Society. We were
not a little astonished, in one of these schools,
to see several Greek priests learning reading
and writing along with the boys; the sight
of these bearded priests, in their sacerdotal
garments, learning their B, a, ba, and twice
one are two, gave us no very high idea of the
state of learning among these self-styled
successors of the apostles. On mentioning
this afterwards to a friend, and expressing my
surprise that persons so grossly ignorant could
be admitted into the priesthood, he said it was
by no means uncommon; that they learn to
repeat the service by rote, and their flocks
neither know nor care about the amount of
their attainments. He told me an anecdote
highly illustrative of the march of intellect in
Greece. On seeing one day, as we did, a
priest in a school among little boys, he entered
into conversation with him ; and learnt, among
other things, that the annual income of many
of the priests is a mere pittance, quite inade-
quate to supply them even with the neces-
saries of life ; that he himself had at one time
only what amounted to about £2. 10s. of our

moncy per annum. My friend asked him
what he did to help out his income : " I kept
a school :" answered he.

Here, for the first time, I beheld the worship
of the Greek Church ; and I was truly astonished at it. The officiating priest was rattling
over the service with a rapidity that rendered
it impossible to hear any articulate sound ; but
in this portion of the service the people took
no part, nor did they give the slightest heed
to it. They came into the church, crossed
themselves, bowed themselves till their faces
nearly touched the ground, got up again,
crossed themselves, and down again, many
times over : they then ran to the pictures on
the wall, crossed and bowed before them, and
then kissed them one after another. I looked
on in utter amazement to see them thus
running about the church like mad people, and
here, again, I asked myself : " Am I in a
Christian land, as it is called, and does this
profess to be Christian worship ?" So much for
my first impressions of what some persons in
England, ignorant of its real character, call
" a sister church."

We left Corfu on the 5th, and reached
Patras on the 6th. From thence we proceeded
towards Athens, and, after a somewhat rough
voyage, arrived there on the 8th. We lost no
time, but went immediately to the Acropolis,
and I was overpowered by the scene; it sur-
passed anything I could have imagined. The
labour and art which are displayed there, and
the massiveness of the structures, all cry aloud,
as it were, and declare the former glory of
Athens. From the Acropolis we proceeded to
Mars' Hill, where Paul stood before the wise
and noble of Athens. Mars' Hill is an ele-
vated rock standing opposite the Acropolis.
From this spot Paul had a full view of all the
splendid buildings that then adorned Athens;
and as he looked on their magnificent temples,
of which the Athenians were justly proud,
"his spirit was stirred in him," when he saw
that these only ministered to their idolatry,
and he said to them : " God that made the
world, and all things therein, seeing that He
is Lord of Heaven and earth, dwelleth not in
temples made with hands."*   It is impossible

* Acts xvii. 24.

to describe the vividness with which this address of Paul's came to my mind; and how very appropriate it is there felt to be. And if he stood there now, what could he say to the Athenians ? Would he not still count them in all things "too superstitious ?" Would he not think their worship only a different form of idolatry; and declare that the God he served is still to them an "unknown God ?"

I looked with the deepest interest on the Corinthian hills, and on the road to Corinth, on which Paul travelled when he departed from Athens. The lively feelings with which we view the spots that have been trodden or inhabited by eminent saints of God, teach us how easily these feelings may grow into idolatry; how easy it is to begin by simply commemorating a saint, and end in worshipping him. But how would all such undue veneration be rebuked by these holy men: "See thou do it not; for I am thy fellow servant."*

We left Athens with much regret, as we

Rev. xxii. 9.

should have enjoyed spending several days
in examining its interesting ruins. On
Sunday the 9th we reached Syra.   We expected to have found public worship there,
in connexion with the Church Missionary
Society; but, owing to the absence of the
Rev. Mr. Hildner, there was none on that
day; we, therefore, returned to the steamer,
where we could enjoy some quiet reading.   I
felt on this, and on many other occasions, the
blessedness of being able, at all times, to enter
within the veil, and to hold communion with
Christ, and with the Church universal, in
heaven and earth.

We left Syra on the 10th, and did not
reach Smyrna until the 12th, at noon, having
been obliged to lay at anchor for twenty-four
hours on account of a high head wind.   On
approaching Smyrna I read the epistle sent
to it by our Saviour, Rev. ii. · Here once
flourished a holy and spiritual church; but
alas! the glory has departed.   Though the
name and the outward forms of Christianity
remain, there is no body of spiritual Christians
to whom the Lord could now say, " I know

thy works, and tribulation, and poverty, but thou art rich."

I called on Mr. Temple, the American missionary; from whom I received an interesting account of Mr. Cohen's labours among the Jews. The late Rev. John Hartley, whom I met at Nice a short time before he fell asleep in Jesus, mentioned to me his having baptised Mr. Cohen, about fourteen years ago, at Constantinople, along with some others of his brethren the Jews. This stirred up great persecution on the part of the unbelieving Jews, who, by bribery and other unworthy means, got their converted brethren thrown into prison. On this, several of the Armenian Christians of Constantinople raised a sum of money among them, to obtain justice for their persecuted Jewish brethren. I may here mention, that, by general testimony, the Armenian is by far the best of the eastern churches; and that body is the only one that takes any interest in the conversion of the Jews. Mr. Hartley had heard nothing of Mr. Cohen for a long time, and desired me to make enquiry about him. Mr. Cohen is

connected with the London Society for promoting Christianity among the Jews ;* and it
was with great pleasure I heard such a favor-
able testimony borne to the faithful labours of
this Christian Jew.

After leaving Mr. Temple, I went to call on
Mr. Barker, the agent of the British and
Foreign Bible Society ; and there I found Mr.
Cohen.   I soon proceeded with him to the
Jewish quarter; and was delighted, indeed, to
find how highly he is respected by the Jews.
The poor come to him to unburden their
hearts, telling him all their griefs, and looking
up to him for counsel with the utmost defe-
rence.   He goes to work in the right way among
his brethren ; living among them, and gaining their affections, by taking a deep interest
in all that concerns them ; thus proving to
them that Christianity is a living principle,
and not a mere system of doctrines.   If we
seek the highest interests of a people, we must
prove to them that we really feel love towards
them ; and this is especially necessary in the

---

* I have since learned that he has left it.

case of the Jews, who have been so much
oppressed by nominal Christians. I am led
to make these remarks by finding a constant
tendency among Christians to trust too ex-
clusively to mere theological argument, as the
only instrument to be used in attempting to
convert the Jews.

Finding that the steamer from Smyrna to
Beyrout would not start for more than a week,
we resolved to occupy the intermediate time
in visiting Constantinople. On the afternoon of
April 14th we went on board the steamer that
was to convey us thither, and soon discovered
most interesting fellow travellers. These
were, Mar Yohannan, a bishop of the Nestorian Christians, three American missionaries,
with their wives, and two female teachers, all
on their way to Persia, to labour among the
Nestorians. One of the missionaries, the
Rev. Justin Perkins, has already laboured
several years among them. Some time since,
he returned to America, accompanied by Mar
Yohannan, who was deputed by the Nestorians
to thank their Christian brethren in America
for what they had already done, and to request

them to send more labourers among them.
This request had been complied with; and
the whole party were now on their return to
Persia. Having been much interested in the
Nestorian Christians by Dr. Grant's account
of them, I felt particularly delighted at this
meeting. When Mr. Perkins introduced me
to Mar Yohannan, I was much struck with his
decidedly Jewish countenance. On shaking
hands with me, he said, in broken English:
" I be a Jew, we be brethren." With this
newly found brother, who seems a sincere
Christian man, I had much interesting conversation. We spoke of their origin. He
said there was no doubt it was Jewish; but
of which tribe he considered doubtful. My
own impression has always been that they
are the descendants of the early Jewish
Christians, the " many thousands of Jews
which believed, and were all zealous of the
law,"* in the days of the apostles; and who
were scattered abroad at the destruction of
Jerusalem. He said it was the opinion of

* Acts xxi. 20.

E

some among them that they are descended
from the Jerusalem Jews. It appears to me
doubtful that the ten tribes will ever be discovered in a body; and scripture does not
lead us to suppose they will be found either
as professing Christians or as Jews; because
it is prophesied of them that they are to serve
the gods of the nations among whom they are
cast out: "The Lord shall scatter thee among
all people, from the one end of the earth even
unto the other; and there thou shalt serve
other gods, which neither thou nor thy fathers
have known, even wood and stone."*   This
must be spoken of the ten tribes; because no
such scattering of the two tribes occurred
until after the destruction of Jerusalem by the
Romans; and, amid all their sins, the two
tribes have never, since their dispersion, been
guilty of worshipping other gods, but have
always viewed idolatry with abhorrence.

Mar Yohannan asked me many questions
about the state of Christianity in England;
particularly as to whether there was much love

* Deut. xxviii. 64.

and Christian union. I explained the nature of the divisions among us ; telling him that all true Christians are agreed in essentials, and only differ on minor points. He asked me whether the bishops allow pious dissenters to preach in the Church of England pulpits; I answered, No ; at which he seemed much grieved, and said : " We let all good ministers preach in our churches." One of his first questions to me, was : " Are you high Church ?" Having satisfied him on this point, he said : " I am glad of it ; I do not like high Church ; high Church will soon become Pope." I asked him to explain what he meant by high Church ; and learnt, from his account, that those views, known in this country as Puseyite or Tractarian, are rapidly spreading among the Episcopalians of America. As this extraordinary heresy is one of the most striking signs of these latter times ; being, as it were, the making " an image to the beast, which had the wound by a sword, and did live,"* it may be worth while to give

Rev. xiii. 14.

my readers some account of its workings in
America ; and the most distinct mode of doing
this will be to give an extract from a work
recently published by Mr. Perkins.

"This modern pharisaism,"* says he, " has
thrust itself upon my attention, in the course
of my visit to the United States, in connexion
with the Nestorian bishop, in instances enough,
if described, to fill a volume, and in a manner
not a little painful to contemplate.   Not long
after our visit to Virginia, an editor of a
religious newspaper in that state sent me a
number, which tells the whole story in a few
words, and from which I give below an extract
to the reader.

'A new Argument for Episcopacy.

'The Rev. Mr. Perkins, and Mar Yohannan,
have recently been on a visit to the friends
of Mr. and Mrs. Holladay, in Virginia.   A
few days ago, the episcopal clergyman, in one

* A Residence of eight years in Persia among the
Nestorian Christians.   By the Rev. Justin Perkins.
Andover, 1843.

of our towns in which they stopped for the
sabbath, importuned the good bishop to attend
his church half of the day, which the stranger
did. The clergyman, in the integrity of his
heart, seized upon the opportunity to make a
glorification of episcopacy, a thing which has
been so repeatedly attempted, in similar circumstances, since Mar Yohannan's arrival in
this country, as not a little to annoy him, as
he himself informs us,—the artless Nestorian,
in his own simple language, having come to
America, not to divide Christians here, but to
hold communion with *all* who love our Lord
Jesus Christ, of whatever name; whereas the
Episcopalians, he adds, always inquire eagerly
of him about the forms and ceremonies of his
church, (the first question uniformly being,
How many orders of the clergy have you,)
while they ask hardly ever a word about the
state of morals or vital religion among his
people.

'But we hasten to the *logic* of the subject.
The Episcopal clergyman in question laboured
to prove to his congregation, in the presence
of Mar Yohannan, that the Nestorians are

Episcopalians; and, as they refer their con-version to Christianity back to the time of the apostles, *therefore,* modern Episcopacy must be apostolic. One link in the ponderous chain of argumentation, leading to this con-clusion, as alluded to by the good clergyman, (and we suppose originated by him) was the resemblance between Mar Yohannan's *cloak* and the Episcopal *robe.* But, unfortunately for the argument, Mar Yohannan's cloak *is the common Persian cloak,* worn alike by all sects and classes in Persia, as Mr. Perkins informs us,—nothing but the bishop's cap in his dress being peculiar and distinctive of his clerical office. * * Oh what a pity that the builders of Christ's spiritual temple, (for such we believe many of our Episcopalian brethren to be) should think so much more of the fabric and fashion of their scaffolding, than of the temple itself! * * How must such zeal for form appear, to an artless mind unaccustomed to it? Listen and see how it does appear. In our town, on the first evening of Mr. Perkins' and Mar Yohannan's arrival here, two Episcopalian clergymen were the first to make their way to their lodgings; and wished the bishop to be at their churches both morning and evening on the sabbath—one of them confidently urging: 'We have a claim, because you belong to us.' 'I do not wish to hear this word,' earnestly replied Mar Yohannan; 'I have not come here to make difference among Christians; I love all who love our Lord Jesus Christ. The name is nothing; but *faith* and *love*; I desire to see all Christians in your happy country love one another: I do not wish to have you say *you belong to us.* We all have one Lord; we will all go to one heaven.' What reply could our worthy Episcopal brother make to this pointed lecture from the artless Nestorian prelate? Not one word.' (From the *Watchman of the South*, May 12th, 1842.)

"While it is much to be lamented," continnes Mr. Perkins, "that a Christian prelate from benighted Asia, should witness such developments of a narrow exclusiveness among Christians in Protestant America, it is matter of unfeigned gratitude to God, that he has not, as we trust, been thus injured. He has been disappointed by it, and often not a little grieved; particularly by some open attacks upon himself in periodicals." Mr. Perkins then quotes a long article from the Churchman, an Episcopal paper, of New York, of which I can only afford room for an extract. "What effect should Mar Yohannan's associating himself with separatists have upon us? If an English bishop came to this country, and, avoiding his legitimate brethren, threw himself into the hands of separatists, what effect would it have on his reception? Has not this bishop, by his intercommunion with separatists, so put himself under the censure of the church, and so violated unity, that he must be put in the same category with those in whose company he is found? And all this will be in accordance with the apostolic canons; the directions of which on these points are: 1st, That heretics shall not be received into communion: 2nd, That no strange bishop shall be received without letters commendatory: 3rd, That those bishops who pray with heretics shall not be received into communion; and those who suffer them to officiate as clergymen shall be deposed. In one or all of these points, Mar Yohannan will certainly be found wanting; and either is sufficient to exclude him from communion." (*The Churchman*, Nov. 12th, 1842.)

Mar Yohannan wrote an answer to these charges, a translation of which is given by Mr. Perkins. It is so full of simplicity and good sense, that I will transcribe the greater part of it, omitting the portion in defence of Nestorius, as being irrelevant to the main subject.

MAR YOHANNAN'S VINDICATION.

"My brethren of the Episcopalians:

"What evil or wicked thing have I wrought in relation to you, that some of you should write about me in your newspapers and scatter them through all America?

"I am one poor man, and my nation is poor. I came to thank Christians in this country for having helped us, and to ask them to help us more, for the name of the Lord Jesus Christ. We are members of one another; if one member suffer, do not all suffer with it? Well, if

you had desired our good, would you not sometimes have inquired of me thus :—What is the
condition of your people in that land of heathens ? Is there a church there ? Are there
good men ? Are there tokens of the influence
of the Holy · Spirit ? What is the state of
knowledge and instruction ? What are the
morals ? But from very few of you have I
heard one of these questions. You ask : *How
many orders have you ?* My friends, forms
are nothing; 'neither is circumcision anything,
nor uncircumcision, but a new creature.'

   " If you say that our church is built upon
the apostolic foundation, the oldest of the
churches, why, shall we place our confidence in
age, name, or forms ? No, but in the Lamb
of God, who descended from His throne on
high to save that which was lost. Observe and
behold ; the Creator of the heights and of the
depths did not demean himself so loftily as
some denominations, who say—*We are ; there
is no other true church.* The Lord said,
Every man who exalteth himself shall be
abased, but whoever humbleth himself shall
be exalted. Again ; your church came out

from the church of the Pope. Is there not
some leaven of the Pope still remaining in
many of you? Take care; if you say 'No,
this word is a mistake,' I have proofs. What
are those pictures in some of your churches?
This is a mark of the Pope. I know you do
not worship the pictures: but your children
who rise up after you, seeing them in the
churches, will worship them. Mark that
second commandment. God said—Thou shalt
not make unto thee any likeness or resemblance
of anything in heaven above, nor in the earth
beneath, nor in the waters under the earth.
Another commandment of God is, Love your
neighbours as yourselves; but you say—*Our
church is great.* Very well; your church has become great, has it? Why? That it may despise
small churches? Our Lord Jesus Christ says,
Whoever will be greatest, let him be *servant*
of all. This haughtiness is another mark of
the Pope, who teaches that none will be saved
who are out of our church.   *   *   *   *   *

"I do not say that your way (church polity) is
not a good one—very good, if you properly
follow it; not in exclusiveness and ostentation,

sayin :—We are *the only true church;* nor in

without, but within full of all uncleanness. God looketh upon the heart. It is important for Christians to abound in love, and not in vain glorying. But every tree is known by its fruit; men also, by their works.

"I love Episcopalians, and Congregationalists, and Presbyterians, and Dutchmen, and Lutherans, and Methodists, and Baptists;— all, as brethren in Christ. There is no difference in them with me. The greater brethren are all these; and if there be less, *we* are the *least.* We open our churches to their priests, and receive them as the priests of God and the apostles of our Lord. Our Lord said—Whosoever receiveth a prophet in the name of a prophet, shall receive a prophet's reward. And whosoever receiveth a righteous man in the name of a righteous man, shall receive a righteous man's reward. Thus have we learned from our Lord.

"You are displeased with me, are you, because I have associated with the Presbyterians and Congregationalists? So the newspaper

teaches. I do not practise partiality. Is it
very strange that I associate most with the
Presbyterians and Congregationalists? No;
they are equally our brethren; and they have
come and helped us, in books and teachers,
and have done a great and good work for our
nation. Ought I to abandon them, and form
new alliances? We do not so understand propriety and justice. Would it not have been a
great wonder, very wrong in me, and very bad
for my nation, had I forsaken them and connected myself with others? It would be a
black reproach, and a great sin for us thus to
abuse the good they have done us. God would
be displeased with us for such a course of
ingratitude. But we will never be unmindful
of their beneficence. We will cling to these
benefactors as we do to Nestorius. Our Lord
Jesus Christ said—Whoever shall give to drink
a cup of cold water shall not lose his reward.
How much greater will be the reward of those
who have given to drink the instructions of
Christ. And shall we abuse the good work
they have done for us? Never. We must
obey God, rather than man; and keep the

commandments of God, rather than the commandments of men.   We all have one Lord,
one faith, one baptism, one God and Father of
our Lord Jesus Christ, who is over all, and in
all ; over us, over you, and over them ; who
will judge us all at the last day, and if found
at his right hand, will raise us all to the same
heaven.   We shall dwell *in peace together*
there.   May the grace of our Lord Jesus
Christ, the love of God the Father, and the
communion of the Holy Spirit, be with us all
for ever.   Amen.

" Your fellow-sinner and unworthy Christian
brother,

"MAR YOHANNAN·"

" *Nov.* 1842."

Mar Yohannan asked me why we did not
send missionaries to the Persian Jews.   I said
that probably we may do so, if God permit.
He said—" Let them be pure and holy men of
God, who will desire to know nothing but
Jesus Christ and Him crucified."

Before taking leave of Mar Yohannan, I
must mention a request of his that amused me

highly. " I have a great favour to ask you,"
said he, "will you promise to grant it to me?"
I replied that I would, if it were in my power
to do so. "It is," said he, "that you would
ask Queen Victoria to write a letter to the King
of Persia, to tell him not to let the Koords
oppress us. We are willing to pay our taxes,
and to live honestly and peaceably; but the
Koords injure and oppress both us and our
uncles, the Jews.* I do not ask Queen Victoria
to send an army; if she will only write to our
King, I am sure he will pay attention to what
she says." It was with much difficulty I could
persuade this simple good man that it was
quite impossible for me to convey any message
to Queen Victoria; however, to pacify him, I
promised that on my return to England I would
publish his request, either in the newspapers,
or in a book, by which means it might meet
the eye of some one who might communicate
it to the Queen. I was much struck by this
simple testimony to the influence of Britain.
If her power were wielded for the glory of God,

* This has been painfully confirmed by the recent
exterminating attack on the hapless Nestorians.

how much good she might accomplish among the nations of the earth!

We arrived at Constantinople about five o'clock in the morning of the 16th April. The view of the city from the water is indeed magnificent. "The first part of the city which meets the view upon entering the Bosphorus from the south, is called Stamboul. Here the massy dome of St. Sophia, and graceful minarets of every kind, crowd upon the sight. Palaces, mosques, and baths, seem to be without number in this renowned capital. And then the rich verdant trees that surround so many of the white marble buildings, and the clear blue sea, which, like a deep full river, laves the shore and flows up the harbour, combine to give Constantinople a gorgeous beauty which is perhaps unrivalled by any city in the world."* The beauty, however, is confined to the view from without. In the interior, the streets are narrow and filthy, infested to a most annoying degree by dogs that belong to no one, but live by what they can pick up in the streets, where

* Narrative of a Mission of Enquiry to the Jews from the Church of Scotland, p. 466.

they remain day and night. Through the day
they are generally asleep, and when roused, or
driven out of the way, are too lazy to bark,
but go to sleep again. I was strongly reminded
by them of the Prophet's description of un-
faithful pastors—" They are all dumb dogs,
they cannot bark; sleeping, lying down, loving
to slumber."* Hateful and disgusting as these
wretched animals are in the eyes of men, how
much more hateful in the sight of a holy God
are selfish and worldly-minded men, who pre-
sume to call themselves pastors of Christ's
flock! At night, these dogs go howling about
the city, exactly according to the description of

make a noise like a dog, and go round about
the city."†

It was on Sunday morning we landed at
Constantinople, and after breakfast one of the
American missionaries, with whom we had tra-

brethren. It was, indeed, a refreshing season
to join in praising our Heavenly Father with

* Isaiah, lvi. 10.　　† Psalm, lix. 6.

these dear brethren, nearly all of whom are
engaged in missionary labour.   I was delighted
to find among them the Rev. Mr. Schwartz,
a Christian Jew, connected with the London
Society for promoting Christianity among the
Jews.*   This "unity of spirit" is indispensable in a missionary to the Jews.   What can
they think of Christianity if they see those
who profess it standing aloof from one another,
or hear one sect of Christian ministers de-
nouncing as "unauthorized teachers" others
who give abundant proof of piety, ability, and
every other requisite for missionary or minis-
terial work ?

Mr. Schwartz labours among the German
Jews in Constantinople, and has much intercourse with them ; and some have been, by his
instrumentality, stirred up to seek the Lord
their God, and Jesus whom He hath sent.

Mr. Schauffler, the American missionary,
devotes himself to the Spanish Jews.   For a
considerable time he met with great opposition.
The chief Rabbi not only excommunicated all

* Now in connexion with the Free Church of Scotland's mission to the Jews.

Jews who dared to visit him, but even probi-
bited any of them from entering the street
where he lived. Since the publication of
Mr. Schauffler's translation of the Bible into
Jewish Spanish, however, the general feeling
of the Jews towards him is much· more
favourable. They feel that he has conferred
a great boon upon them, and his translation
of the Bible is much sought after by them.

In walking through the streets of Constantinople, I was much struck with the dress of the
Turkish women. They wear a handkerchief
bandaged over the forehead, and another over
the nose, and lower part of the face, so that
nothing but the eyes is seen. This forcibly
reminded me that, though still in Europe, I
was now in a city where Christianity is openly
denied. The degradation of the females which
prevails in Mohammedan as well as heathen
countries, shows how much women owe to that
divine revelation which declares that "in
Christ Jesus there is neither male nor female."

The slave market is another proof how far
behind the rest of Europe Turkey is in civili-

zation. The chief part of the business appeared to be over when I visited it, as there were only a few young women and boys left. The purchasers went up to these poor creatures, felt their arms, and examined them as one would examine cattle. The merely animal expression of their countenances bespoke the lowest state of mental degradation, and gave an awful picture of what corrupt human nature can do; that man should bring his fellow-creature, with a soul as immortal as his own, to the level of the brutes that perish! If we feel indignant at a Turk for doing this, what shall we say to men calling themselves Christians, who venture to defend a system so horrible!

On the 22nd we returned to Smyrna, and on the 23rd went to the morning service at the English chapel. Before relating what I saw and heard there, I must make a remark which applies not only to this, but to every future occasion on which I may see it right to notice the doings of churches or religious societies. In these days of division and party strife, a lover of peace is strongly tempted to let things alone, and pass over in silence what he cannot notice with approbation. This is rather to consult his own ease and safety, than the advancement of Christ's kingdom. Besides, does it not really savour of a sectarian spirit to say, " I do not belong to the Church of England; its doings are no business of mine?" If we feel that we belong to the church of Christ, the proceedings of every section of that church must be interesting to us, and must be either painful or pleasing, as we consider them in harmony with, or contrary to, the mind of God. I believe the time is come when all false delicacy must be laid aside, and the truth spoken out, as unto the Lord, and not unto men. What might have been considered a few years ago as a piece of isolated absurdity, can now be viewed in no other light than part of a widely extended plan to restore the errors of Popery.

The building which has for some years been used as a place of worship in Smyrna, in connexion with the Church of England, was on this day consecrated, as it is called, by the Bishop of Gibraltar. When the congregation were assembled, the Bishop entered, carrying a silver staff on his arm, about the size of an ordinary poker, on the top of which was a cross. He walked up to the communion table, followed by three ministers in surplices, and laid the silver staff on the table where the communion vessels were set out for show, the Lord's supper not being dispensed on that day. Having done this, he and his attendants walked back again to the door, where they faced about, and walked again towards the altar, the Bishop repeating: "Open to me the gates of righteousness," and the rest of the service prescribed for the occasion. Now I will ask any candid member of the Church of England, whether this silly apeing of Popish ceremonies is expedient in places where hitherto Christianity has been seen only through the medium of Romish and Greek churches. Should not the great aim of Protestant Christians be, not thus to identify themselves with Popery, but to show that their Christianity is something very different from it?

On Monday, the 24th of April, about three o'clock in the morning, we left Smyrna in an

Austrian steamer for Beyrout. The accommodation was good, and the weather very favourable ; the only discomfort we felt was from the
crowded state of the deck, which was nearly
filled with passengers. These were chiefly
Turks, and a great part of their time was spent
in acts of devotion. Each one, every time he
prayed, took out a little pocket compass, to
ascertain in what direction Mecca lay, that he
might turn his face towards it. Their devo-
tions consisted chiefly in bending many times
to the ground, raising the ears with the
thumbs, which a fellow-passenger explained
to me meant lifting up their ears for an answer
to their prayers ; and turning their faces to the
right and left, which I was told is to frighten
away the evil spirits. The concluding ceremony was stroking the face and beard several
times, which was said to signify the wiping
away of sin. When the wind got up a little
they went through all these movements with
redoubled earnestness. A person on board
asked one of them why he prayed so much ;
he replied, because the wind blew, and he was
afraid. If Christianity does not present to us

a living, spiritual reality, but only sends us to rites and ceremonies for comfort, wherein is it better than Mohammedanism, or any other false religion? If Protestantism does not manifest the clearest gospel light in the midst of those so devoted to forms, her colonial establishments will be little else than " darkness visible."

About three o'clock in the afternoon the captain pointed out to us the Isle of Patmos. The weather being very fine, we were enabled to go close by it; and a ruin was pointed out to us which is said to be that of the prison where John was confined. Whether this were the case or not mattered little to me; there was the island itself, where our blessed Saviour appeared to the beloved disciple, and I viewed it with the deepest emotion. To this lonely and desolate spot, far removed from his brethren and children in the gospel, was John banished, " for the word of God and for the testimony of Jesus Christ."*   Here was no consecrated building, no outward ordinance; but here the Lord met him, and communed with him; and

* Rev. i. 9.

the barren rock was indeed consecrated ground
to John. My recent visit to Smyrna, one of
the churches to which Jesus sent a message
from hence, led me to think of the tenor of the
charges delivered by this the true Bishop of
souls. Does He speak to the churches of government or of ritual? Does he reprove them
for inattention to outward forms, or exhort
them to the observance of times and seasons?
No; the inward life in the soul, and its outward manifestations in walk and conversation,
are the only subjects on which he touches.
" I have somewhat against thee, because thou
hast left thy first love." " I know thy works
that thou hast a name that thou livest, and art
dead." " Thou sayest, I am rich, and increased with goods, and have need of nothing;
and knowest not that thou art wretched, and
miserable, and poor, and blind, and naked."
Alas! who can listen to the tone of gratulation
in which too many sections of the church speak
of their state, without being reminded of this
address to the church of Laodicea; and fearing
that if our Bishop and Head of the Church now

G

sent a message to professing Christendom, it would be couched in the same language!

How many thoughts crowded on my mind as I gazed on this barren and desolate island! The wonderful vision vouchsafed to John,— the chart of prophecy displayed to him,— the awful and glorious things that " shall be here- after ;" things still future, yet perhaps not far distant! Oh how speedily man's silly inventions and vain speculations fall before a believing view of " the root and offspring of David, the bright and morning star!" We need no officiating priest, no abstractive called *the church*, to bring us into communion with God. " The spirit and the bride say come, and let him that is athirst come; and whosoever will, let him take the water of life freely." How blessed, to the humble Christian, these latest revelations of the Divine mind, authoritatively promulgated on this lonely rock! And how awful the threatening that sums them up! " If any man shall add unto these things, God shall add unto him the plagues that are written in this book." Is not " unwritten tradition," of which we now hear so much, somewhat like an addition to God's words?

On Tuesday, the 25th, we landed at Rhodes, where the apostle Paul touched on his way from Ephesus to Jerusalem. The town looked dull and deserted ; but this was accounted for by our being told it was on that day a feast of the Greek church, and that the greater part of the inhabitants had gone out of the town to make merry. The British Consul kindly sent his dragoman with us, to show us the street of the knights. I soon discovered that our guide was a Jew, and learnt from him that there are between two and three hundred Jewish families in the place. The street of the knights is a long narrow street, with old houses on each side, on the walls of which are carved the arms of the knights who were engaged in the crusades. These our guide pointed out to us; and added, contemptuously, pointing to an image of the Virgin—" That is the figure of a woman."

Before we left Rhodes, a number of Jews and Jewesses came on board the steamer to look at the machinery, who were courteously

received by the captain.   It was interesting to
me to see so many of my nation; and curious
to observe, in the dress of the women, the
same love of wearing ornaments that existed
among them of old.   Some of the children
had their foreheads covered with little gold
coins threaded on a string, which had a very
odd appearance.

We left Rhodes the same evening; and on
the 27th, about noon, arrived at Cyprus.
Here I was again reminded of Paul; and,
also of Barnabas, who was a native of Cyprus.
Although this island is very fertile, every
thing about it has the appearance of poverty
and desolation.   It is now very thinly inhabited; and large tracts of land are nncul-
tivated.   We are told that land can be
purchased at from two to four shillings an
acre.   I could not help wishing that some of
our starving population of England were trans-
ported hither, to cultivate the land that lies
waste.   There are no Jews in the island of
Cyprus.

On the morning of the 28th we landed at
Beyrout.   I was very kindly received by the

American missionaries; the Rev. Eli Smith invited me to stay in his house, where I was much refreshed in spirit by prayer and conversation with these dear brethren. As I paid a longer visit to this place on my return from Palestine, I shall reserve the account of it until my second visit.

We left Beyrout on the 2nd of May, accompanied by other three travellers. We were now obliged to perform all our journeys on horseback; the roads in Syria, if roads they may be called, being quite unfit for carriages of any kind. Soon after leaving Beyrout we began to ascend the mountains of Lebanon, and continued ascending for seven or eight hours. The change from the warm climate of Beyrout to the cold air of the mountain ridge was very great. When we got to the height of about 6000 feet, we began to descend the other side of the ridge; and at seven o'clock we arrived at Aksah, a small village in the plain that lies between the ridges of Lebanon and Anti-Lebanon. This village consists of a few mud hovels, into the largest of which we were admitted for the night; the

family who inhabited it going to sleep in the
stable to make room for us.   After a fatiguing
ride on horseback of fourteen hours, I hoped
to enjoy a refreshing sleep; but in this I was
sadly disappointed.   To convey an adequate
idea of the combined annoyances of our apartment, would be a vain attempt.   The room
was so filled with the smoke of cow-dung,
(which when dried is used for fuel) that we
could not see any thing at a yard distant.
After taking a little food, we spread our mats
on the floor, and lay down to rest, as we fondly
hoped; but, alas! no sooner had we settled
ourselves, than such a fierce onset was commenced by the tiny inhabitants of the place,
that all the previous assaults made on us in
Italy and elsewhere, were as nothing in comparison.   In a little time I heard sundry
strange noises in the room; and being unable
to sleep, I got up, and took a light to examine
what sort of companions we might have in the
apartment that was professedly given up solely
to our use.   In one corner I found a calf; in
another, a sick goat; over our heads, pigeons;
and to complete the company, a cat with a

litter of kittens. In the morning when we
were dressing, we were greatly annoyed by the
women of the house, and some of their neighbours, coming to the door to look at the
strangers; appearing quite unconscious that
there was the slightest impropriety in their
doing so.

We were but little refreshed by our night's
lodgment, for *rest* it could not be called; and
on first setting out on our journey we suffered
much from the cold. Our route lay through
the plain of Bekaa, which is beautifully situated
between the two lofty mountain ridges; and
the snowy top of Hermon was in our view all
day. In the evening we arrived at Baalbec;
and finding the ground still too damp for
pitching our tent, we took up our abode in
the convent.

Baalbec is the ancient Heliopolis, and the
Baaleth* of Scripture, built by Solomon. It
contains the ruins of magnificent buildings in
the Grecian style; but when, or by whom,
erected, is unknown. The remains of the

* 2 Chron. viii. 6.

Temple of the Sun are a wonderful monument of the power of man. Some of the pillars of the portico remain, which are upwards of 70 feet in height ; but the most extraordinary part of it is the great size of the stones in the sloping wall around the raised platform on which the temple stood. Many of them are from 30 to 35 feet in length ; and at one corner are three enormous stones, each of them about sixty feet in length. There is one stone still lying in the quarry close by, hewn out on three sides ; this M. measured, and found it of the amazing dimensions of $66\frac{1}{2}$ feet long,* by 13 feet in breadth, and the same in thickness. The framers of these great works doubtless thought that their names would be handed down to the latest posterity ; but their memory is perished. At present not only man' greatest, but even his meanest works, outlive himself ; but God hath said that in the days when He will " Rejoice in Jerusalem and joy in his people," his chosen " Shall wear out the work of their hands."†

---

* I find that Volney, quoted by Keith, makes the length 69 feet 2 inches.   † Isaiah lxv. 22—*margin.*

We left Baalbec on Friday the 5th, and arrived at Damascus about 3 o'clock in the afternoon of the 6th. The journey on the second day was very unpleasant; the heat was great; the glare of light from the white rocks was painful to the eyes; and the ascent up the stony hill, near the city, steep and difficult. After all these disagreeables, one is much delighted, on reaching the summit of this hill, with the first view of Damascus, as it lies stretched out below, interspersed with trees and gardens. In travelling through Syria and Palestine the aspect of all around is generally so cheerless and desolate, that any appearance of verdure and cultivation is doubly welcome, and strikes the eye by the effect of contrast, in a way the same scenery would never do if seen in any part of Europe. It is only in this way that I can account for the glowing descriptions of the Bible; in every thing that one sees, recalling to mind some ancient custom, and almost every locality being connected with some important or interesting event.

Here I was in Damascus, the oldest existing city in the world; probably founded soon after the dispersion at Babel. The steward of Abraham's house was " Eliezer of Damascus." Amid all the revolutions of empires, and the overthrow of mighty cities in the east and in the west, here stands Damascus still; a city associated with Elisha, Ahaz, and Rezin! It existed before the call of Abraham, and survived the dispersion of the Jewish nation; it stood at the coming of our Lord in humiliation, and may continue till his second coming in glory.

But its more ancient associations did not long detain me from meditating on its connexion with that wonderful man who was rightly accused of " turning the world upside down ;" and to whose instrumentality the present state of Europe, as the centre of civilization, may be traced. When Saul, "yet breathing out threatenings and slaughter,'' set out on his

journey to Damascus, he little thought of the
mighty change that awaited him ere he should
reach this ancient city. " As he journeyed
he came near Damascus ; and suddenly there
shined round about him a light from heaven ;
and he fell to the earth, and heard a voice
saying unto him, Saul, Saul, why persecutest
thou me?* The fierce persecutor of Jesus
at once becomes His docile follower—" Lord,
what wilt thou have me to do?" is the rule of
his life from that day forward ; and Saul of
Tarsus is indeed " a new creature."

Such is regeneration, needful not only to the
open opposer of religion, but to every son of
Adam,—to every possessor of that " carnal
mind" which is " enmity against God." And
though we look not for a visible light to shine
aroundt he awakened sinner, yet must the light
of the glorious gospel shine into his heart," to
give the light of the knowledge of the glory of
God in the face of Christ Jesus;"† in order
that he may " put off concerning the former
conversation, the old man, which is corrupt

* Acts, ix, 3, 4.　　　　† 2 Cor. iv. 6.

according to the deceitful lusts, and be renewed in the spirit of his mind, and put on the new man which after God is created in righteousness and true holiness."*

The teaching of our Lord and His apostles is full of this important doctrine; of the necessity of this great change " from darkness to light, and from the power of Satan unto God." And yet there are men calling themselves ministers of the gospel of Christ who represent this mighty change as taking place in an unconscious infant, in consequence of an outward ceremony! It is, indeed, a subtle device of Satan to persuade men that they are already "members of Christ, children of God, and inheritors of the kingdom of heaven," while they are yet in the " gall of bitterness, and in the bond of iniquity." While " the whole head is sick, and the whole heart faint," he tells them that they are among " the whole," who need no physician; and thus prevents them from applying to the Great Physician who alone is able to heal their spiritual disease.

* Eph. iv. 22—24.

He who has personally experienced this blessed change is not likely to imagine it took place in his baptism, nor to value himself on having " kept the white robe of baptism unde-filed ;"* he knows what sin is, and what real purity of heart is, too well, to mistake the re-straints of education and society for that " holi-ness, without which no man shall see the Lord." Rather will he be disposed to exclaim, as Paul did on reviewing his state previous to his conversion, " What things were gain to me, those I counted loss for Christ : yea doubt-less, and I count all things but loss for the excellency of the knowledge of Christ Jesus, my Lord."†

Damascus, like all other towns in Syria, is a dirty, disagreeable place. We took up our abode in what is called a European Hotel, and flattered ourselves we should be free from the usual Oriental annoyance of vermin ; but so far was this from being the case, that our room contained scorpions, in addition to the usual varieties of invaders. When I was in Italy, I thought nothing could exceed the filth and dis-

* Pusey on Baptism, p. 53.　　† Phil. iii. 7, 8.

comfort of Italian inns : but a very short sojourn in Syria led me to see that no part of
Europe is quite so low in the scale of cleanli-
ness.

We visited several of the houses of the
wealthy Jews, and were received with the
utmost kindness and courtesy by the ladies of
the family, the gentlemen being from home.
Their houses are very handsome, and are built
and furnished in the usual eastern style.   On
entering the door from the street, you do not
go into the house, but into a large square
court, round which the different apartments
are situated.   In some of these courts there is
a reservoir of water in the centre, planted round
with orange and lemon trees.   The room in
which the ladies received us was large and
lofty; the ceiling highly ornamented with
painting and gilding, and the walls similarly
decorated, and hung with looking glasses. The
lower end of the room, into which you first
enter, is paved with marble; this may occupy
about a third of the apartment, the remainder
consists of a platform about a foot and a half
high, covered with a Turkey carpet, or, in some

instances, with fine matting. Round three
sides of this platform there is a farther eleva-
tion, about a foot or more in height, and about
the width of an ordinary sofa, called the *divan*;
and on this the family and their guests sit, or
rather recline. The divan is covered with
damask, or with the richest Persian car-
peting.

The dress of the ladies was very splendid;
they wore loose eastern robes of silk, with a sort
of breastplate or stomacher covered with gold,
and jewelled ornaments on their heads. Their
manners were affable and pleasing. They regaled
us with coffee and sweetmeats, with the usual ac-
companiment of pipes, or nargilas. The nargila,
which is like the Indian hookah, consists of a
glass vessel full of water, that stands on the
floor, through which the smoke is made to
pass ; it is inhaled through a long flexible tube,
having a mouthpiece. I was very awkward in
the use of this machine, (which it would have
been esteemed very uncivil to decline,) and
could not get it to smoke at all, which one of
the young ladies of the family perceiving, with
a good-humoured smile at my awkwardness,

took the mouthpiece out of my hand, and after
two or three good whiffs, put it in smoking
trim, and returned it to me.

I made inquiries as to the state of female
education among the Jews; and was surprised
to find that in many of the wealthiest families
the daughters were unable to read. I am surprised that Sir Moses Montefiore, who takes
such an interest in our brethren, has not effected some improvement in this matter.

I must not omit to mention one decoration
of the ladies, which, though in my opinion
it rather marred their beauty, yet afforded an
interesting illustration of Scripture. From the
outer corner of each eye a black line is painted
upon the cheek, which gives the appearance of
two slits or rents. This explains Jer. iv. 30,
" Though thou rendest thy eyes*with painting
in vain shalt thou make thyself fair."

These ladies, as well as all the Jews I saw
in Damascus, expressed their gratitude to the
English for the kind interest they had taken
in the sufferers during the recent persecution.

* This is the literal translation of the Hebrew ; see
the margin.

Most of my readers will remember that a certain Father Thomaso, a Roman Catholic priest,
suddenly disappeared ; and the Romanists at
Damascus immediately accused the Jews of
having murdered him, in order to obtain his
blood for the celebration of the passover. It
was in vain the Jews protested their innocence,
and that they never use blood at the passover.
Many of the most wealthy and respectable
Jews were cast into prison, and inhumanly
flogged in order to induce them to confess
their guilt. Not content with this, the government had even the barbarity to cause a number
of the Jewish children to be flogged, in the
expectation of extorting some confession from
them. Four Jews died in consequence of this
torture and imprisonment ; and it is probable
that many others would have fallen victims to
Popish and Mohammedan cruelty, had it not
been for the interest taken by the English nation at large in the persecuted Jews, and the
efforts of Sir Moses Montefiore.

This is by no means a solitary instance of
the persecuting spirit the Romanists manifest

against the Jews in the east; several instances
of similar attempts to criminate the Jews were
mentioned to me, from which I select only one.
A young woman, a Roman Catholic, disappeared
from Sidon, and her relatives and the other
Romanists began immediately to accuse the
Jews of having murdered her.   Providentially
for my poor brethren, the Prussian Vice-Consul
at Beyrout made some investigation into the
matter, and discovered that she had eloped
with a priest!   I must once and again remind
Christians of what I do not think they take
sufficiently into account,—the effect which
such exhibitions of the Christisn religion,
(falsely so called) have upon the minds of the
Jews.   They are persecuted both by the Greek
and Romish churches; and these two churches
are the chief specimens of Christianity that in
the East are presented before them.   Can any
thing, therefore, be more grossly absurd than
that members of a Protestant church, who go
to the East for the express purpose of converting the Jews to Christianity, should seek in
any way to assimilate themselves to those cor-

rùpt churches, instead of using every endeavour to show that they are in all respects different from them !"*

We spent one Lord's day in Damascus, and it was melancholy to think that in the city where Paul first "preached the faith which once he destroyed," there was not a Christian church with which we could worship. I trust there are many of those, who, for the sake of supporting a theory, maintain that the Romish and Greek churches, though corrupt, are still churches of Christ, who would shrink from acting consistently with this profession by joining in their worship, even where no other offered. For my own part, I do not hesitate to say that I do not reckon them churches of Christ at all; they are heathenism, mixed up with certain Christian dogmas, that become completely neutralized by the mixture. The one Mediator between God and man, the one

* Since the above was written, the Rev. Messrs. Graham and Allen have been sent by the Free Church of Scotland, as missionaries to the Jews in Damascus. I rejoice to think that from these excellent men my brethren will hear Gospel truth in all its purity.

only mode of a sinner's justification,—all, in short, that is peculiarly Christian, is virtually denied in these churches. In addition to this, the mode of worship in the Greek church is so absolutely foolish, that I could much more easily join in the worship of a Jewish synagogue.

In these circumstances, it is delightful to realize the promise of our gracious Saviour, that even when there are but *two* met together in His name He is with them.

We left Damascus on the morning of May 9th. The road was dreary and desolate ; and after a ride of eight hours, we arrived at the village of Sasa. It presented the usual forlorn appearance of an Arab village, and its wild inhabitants looked like savages.

Here for the first time we pitched our tent. The tents used in the East differ little from those that are common in this country, only that, instead of being white, or nearly so, they are composed of alternate stripes of yellow and blue, or some other contrasted colours. The spot were we pitched was very unpleasant, our flooring being composed of dry mud ;

but we could get no better near the village. It was very interesting to me thus to "dwell in a tent," like my forefathers. It excites a lively remembrance that "here we have no continuing city, but seek one to come;" even a "city that hath foundations," as opposed to an assemblage of tents pitched on the surface of the ground. It was delightful to reflect, that the same God who watched over my fathers in all their journeys is my God, who will guide me by His counsel through all my pilgrimage here, and afterwards receive me into glory.

In the evening, as we sat in our tent, we heard a loud crying and howling, as of some one in great distress. We ran out to see what was the matter, and found the noise proceeded from a Bedouin, whom our muleteers had bound hand and foot; they found him lurking about our tent, and supposed he came there to steal. At our desire they let him go, and we had no farther molestation.

The next morning we struck our tent at an early hour, and set out on our journey. The ride to-day was rather more agreeable, there being some little appearance of vegetation oc-

casionally to relieve the eye. A few dwarf
oaks and thorn bushes were a welcome sight
amid the general desolation. About four o'clock
P. M. we arrived at the village of Kuneitirah, if
village it may be called, consisting only of a
few mud hovels and Bedouin tents. It is
rather prettily situated, and is surrounded by
cultivated fields, and flocks of sheep and goats
feeding. It is impossible to give an idea of the
pleasure derived from the sight of a little cultivation in this barren land, on which the curse
of God so evidently rests. " He turneth rivers
into a wilderness, and the water springs into
dry ground ; a fruitful land into barrenness,
for the wickedness of them that dwell therein."*
This has been fulfilled to the very letter ; shall
we not then confidently expect the great and
mighty change both on the land and the
people, that is so frequently predicted ?   " Is
it not yet a very little while that Lebanon shall
be turned into a fruitful field, and the fruitful
field shall be esteemed as a forest ? And in
that day shall the deaf hear the words of the

* Psalms, cvii. 33, 34.

book, and the eyes of the blind shall see out of obscurity, and out of darkness."*

After our tent was pitched, a number of Bedouins came and sat down at our tent door, looking at us with much curiosity and interest. My friend M. took out his six-barrelled pistol for their amusement, and fired off the percussion caps. They listened to the successive reports with astonishment, and lifting up their hands said—" It is from heaven." Such are their notions of a heavenly gift! I happened to make use of a Pisa match, which is ignited by merely pinching one end of it. This also delighted them. "It is magic," they cried out.

The next morning we again set out at an early hour. The scenery was more agreeble, and the soil more fertile, than any we had hitherto seen in this quarter. It was melancholy to see thousands of acres lying waste, and the country lonely and depopulated. " If ye walk contrary to me," said the Lord to my forefathers, "your highways shall be desolate."†

* Isaiah, xxix. 17, 18.　　† Levit. xxvi. 21, 22.

" I scattered them with a whirlwind among all
the nations whom they knew not. Thus the
land was desolate after them, that no man
passed through nor returned, for they laid the
pleasant land desolate."* The people to whom
the Lord gave it are far away, and the few
strangers that are scattered up and down in it
do not seem at home. It yet waits for the
time when "He that scattered Israel will gather
him, and keep him as a shepherd doth his
flock ;"† and then will the promise be fulfilled,
"Thy waste and thy desolate places, and the
land of thy destruction shall even now be too
narrow by reason of .the inhabitants, and they
that swallowed thee up shall be far away."‡

After riding about four hours, we came in
sight of the Lake of Tiberias. It was deeply
interesting to behold s spot so intimately connected with the history of our blessed Lord.
This is that " sea of Galilee, which is the sea
of Tiberias,"§ and which is elsewhere called
the Lake of Gennesaret."‖ On the borders
of this lake stood the towns of Bethsaida and

* Zech. vii. 14.   † Jer. xxxi. 10.
‡ Isaiah, xlix. 19.   § John, vi. 1.   ‖ Luke, v. 1.

places" were often resorted to by Jesus for the purpose of private devotion.

After travelling an hour and a half more, we crossed the river Jordan, by the Jisr Benat Yacob, that is, the bridge of the daughters of Jacob. Tradition says that this is the place where Jacob crossed the Jordan on his return from Mesopotamia, and where his gratitude was called forth at the remembrance of all the mercies the Lord had bestowed upon him. "With my staff I passed over this Jordan, and now I am become two bands."*

Hitherto we had been only on the east of Jordan, in that portion of the land that was the inheritance of the two tribes and a half, but now we were really within the promised land, "the good land that is beyond Jordan." Here we rested for an hour, and took our mid-day meal, drinking, for the first time, of the water of Jordan. As we proceeded on our journey, we met several camels and asses laden with goods, which strongly reminded us of Scripture times.

* Gen. xxxii, 10.

Finding we could not reach the town of
Tiberius that evening, we pitched our tent near
the lake, between the supposed sites of Bethsaida and Capernaum. Of these two cities,
against which our Lord denounced a "woe,"
not a vestige remains, and the places where
they once stood are a mere matter of conjecture. As I meditated on that sure word of
prophecy, and saw its exact fulfilment, I could
not help applying the like warning to Christendom at the present day; and of all parts
of Christendom, to highly-favoured England.
No other land possesses so much of gospel
light; yet how many therein are hating that
light, and refusing to walk in it !

This was an interesting resting-place; as,
though the precise sites cannot be ascertained,
there is no doubt that in this immediate neigh-
bourhood were "the cities wherein most of His
mighty works were done,"* who came to be
" a light to lighten the Gentiles, and the glory
of His people, Israel." Yet, alas ! Israel is
not yet gathered, and of the Gentiles there is

* Mat. xi. 20.

but a little band that are His followers. As I
walked by the lake, one of the first objects
that caught my eye, was an Arab Musselman
praying, with his face towards Mecca. How
wonderful, that in the mysterious providence
of God the religion of Mahomet, the false
prophet, has been permitted to spread far more
widely than the religion of His well-beloved
Son! "Go into all the world, and proclaim
the good news to every creature," was the
command of Jesus to His disciples. The first
disciples obeyed, and many were added to the
church. Satan, finding his empire invaded,
accomplished his highest device, that of getting
the world introduced into that which was called
the Church of Christ, and thus he brought in
the confusion that has continued in the visible
church, even to the present time. The good
news ceased to be proclaimed; man's inventions made the word of God of none effect,
and the dominion of error prevailed far and
wide.

And the followers of the false prophet now
rule in the land that God gave to his chosen
people; the land where Jesus dwelt, and com-

municated the light of truth, and from whence
He sent forth His disciples into all the world.
When we look at the unbroken ranks of Ma-
hometanism, and remember how few are disposed to listen to that which involves the
penalty of a violent death, (it being a capital
crime in a Mahometan to forsake his religion,)
we should be disposed to despair of any better
state of things, were it not for the sure word
of prophecy on which God hath caused us to
hope,—" I have sworn by Myself, the word is
gone out of my mouth in righteousness, and
shall not return, that unto Me every knee shall
bow, every tongue shall swear."*

The lake of Tiberias, where several of our
Lord's disciples followed their calling as fishermen, still abounds in fish. We saw a man
wade into the water a little way, and throw in
a small hand net, which he soon brought out
filled with fish. I thought of Jesus, who,
when "walking by the sea of Gallilee, saw two
brethren, Simon called Peter, and Andrew his
brother, casting a net into the sea, for they

* Isaiah, xlv. 23.

were fishers. And He saith unto them, follow Me, and I will make you fishers of men."* Peter the humble fisherman, became Peter the humble and self-denying apostle. My mind involuntarily wandered to his professed successor, with his Swiss guards and regal pomp, and to the statue that bears his name, to which idolatrous honours are paid. What would have been the feelings of this godly " elder," had it been revealed to him that he should in after ages receive the homage due to Christ alone!

On this side of the lake there are a few trees to be seen, a rare and welcome sight in Palestine; we were also much struck with the quantity of rhododendrons of large size, and in full flower, that grew near where we had pitched our tent. And when some of the fish we had just seen caught were broiled for our repast, the scenes of Scripture times came vividly before us.

When we first arrived at the lake, it was perfectly calm; but shortly after our tent was

* Mat. iv. 18, 19.

pitched the wind suddenly arose, and blew so strongly that we had some difficulty in keeping the tent from being blown away. The surface of the lake rose in large waves, so that we could quite understand the gospel narrative, that when " Jesus went into a ship with his disciples there came down a storm of wind on the lake; and they were filled with water, and were in jeopardy."*

In the morning we bathed in the clear waters of the lake, and felt much refreshed. We set out towards Tiberias about half-past six o'clock, and arrived there soon after eleven. The town looked a heap of ruins. It is situated close to the lake, and was formerly surrounded, except on the side next the water, by a high wall, but the great earthquake of 1837 threw it down, as well as most of the houses. Besides this calamity, it was visited by the plague about two years since, and many of the inhabitants died of it.

We took up our abode in the house of a Jew, and in the course of the day I saw and

* Luke, viii. 22, 23.

conversed with many of my poor brethren.
The Jewish population suffered severely in the
plague, nearly a third of them, according to
the information of our host, having died of it.
Those that remain are generally very poor, the
greater number of them living in tents. Ti-
herias is one of the four cities which are
reckoned holy by the Jews, the other three
being Jerusalem, Saphet, and Hebron. The
Jewish population of these cities is on this
account replenished from time to time with
Jews from Europe, chiefly from Germany and
Russia, who come to live, or, in many in_
stances, to die, in one of the holy cities.

In the evening we took a walk towards the
little assemblage of tents that forms the chief
portion of the Jewish quarter. It was Friday
evening, the commencement of the Jewish
Sabbath. We heard in every direction the
voice of prayer; they had just returned from
the synagogue, and were pronouncing the
prayers on the cup of blessing at their evening
meal. We saw one venerable looking old
rabbi, dressed in a white robe, and having a
white beard, and several other rabbis with him,

who were strangers that had come to spend their Sabbath in Tiberias. He performed the ceremony with a great deal of solemnity and feeling; and it was interesting to see him consecrating the bread before he cut it in pieces and divided it among the family and guests. I could not help crying unto the Lord, speedily to make known to poor Israel that Bread of life that came down from heaven, of which if a man eat he shall never die.

The lake of Tiberias is about twelve miles long, and six miles broad at its widest part. It is surrounded by hills; in some places these rise abruptly from the water, and in others retire further back, leaving some level ground by the side of the lake. The river Jordan may be said to run through it, as it enters it on the north, and issues from it again at the southern extremity; taking its course from thence to the Dead Sea. The town of Tiberias is situated on the western side of the lake, as was also Capernaum. Whenever our Saviour is spoken of as being by the sea side, or as crossing the sea, this locality is meant. It may therefore be supposed how deeply interesting it is to the

Christian to feel that he is really in the very
place where his beloved Lord dwelt, and
taught, and wrought miracles. In those places
that have only traditional authority to rest
upon, one has always the feeling that this may
be the spot, or it may not; and this doubt
destroys the interest; but the grand features
of nature are unchangeable, and in looking on
the sea of Gallilee you know that you behold
the very lake which Jesus so often crossed on
errands of mercy, on the surface of which He
walked, and the waves whereof He rebuked
and stilled into a calm. On looking across
from Tiberias you know that you see the
country of the Gadarenes, where He cast out
the legion of unclean spirits. " Being told
that on the coast directly opposite, where the
hills seemed very steep, and close upon the
ₗwaᵗerₚ there were many tombs cut out of the
rocks, our desire was excited more than ever to
cross the lake, for we were sure that the opposite side was ' the country of the Gaderenes,
which is over against Galilee.' From a com_
parison of all the circumstances, it seemed
likely that the scene of the amazing miracle

wrought upon the man possessed by legion was
directly opposite, and that the steep place of
which they spoke might possibly be the hill
down which the herd of swine ran violently
into the sea."*

'On the same eastern side of the lake also
was the " desert place" where our Lord mira-
culously fed the multitude.   Alas! how desert
are all the places there now!   I thought of the
boats of the fishermen of Bethsaida and Capernaum, and of the " other boats" that came
from Tiberias, as I looked on the wide expanse
of the lake, where not a single boat is to be
seen.   We were told there is only one boat on
the whole lake, but we did not see even this
one.   "I will make your cities waste, and I
will bring the land into desolation."†

Our Jewish landlord was suffering severely
from the common disease of the country,
ophthalmia.   On the evening we arrived I ad-
ministered some simple remedies to him, and
in the morning he was so much better that he
knew not how to express his gratitude.   He

* Narrative of a mission of Enquiry to the Jews from
the Church of Scotland.   † Levit. xxvi. 31, 32.

kissed my hand many times, and thanked me in the most fervent manner. This led me to see how desirable it is, since the gift of healing has ceased in the Christian church, that every missionary station should have a medical man attached to it, that those who come to introduce the religion of Jesus may imitate him as far as they can in going about healing all manner of sickness. Where the two can be united in one person it is better still, as the medical missionary can obtain access where the visits of another missionary would not be received.* It is very melancholy to see the ravages of disease in Syria, in cases where there is every reason to believe timely medical aid would effect a cure. I was much struck in Damascus to see so many persons, in the prime of life, totally blind. In that large city there is not a single medical man.

* A society has lately be organized in London, called the " Syrian Medical Aid Association," for the purpose of sending pious physicians to Syria, who may minister both to soul and body. We had much intercourse with their excellent agent, Dr. Kerns, at Beyrout. It is to be hoped that British liberality will enable them soon to increase the number of their agents.

On the morning of Saturday, May 13, we
left Tiberias for Nazareth. As we drew near
Mount Tabor, we sent on the servants with
the luggage, and took the guide we had hired
at Tiberias to conduct us to the the top of it.
After we had ascended the mountain a little
way, we found the place to which he had
brought us steep, rugged, and all but im-
passible; and we then discovered that our
guide, like too many who take on themselves
the office of religious guides, knew nothing of
the way in which he professed to lead us, never
having ascended the mountain himself. We
had therefore nothing for it but to clamber up
to the top the best way we could, which at
length we succeeded in doing.

Mount Tabor is a detached mountain, rising
about a thousand feet above the plain. It has,
ever since the fourth century, had the reputa-
tion of being the mount of transfiguration;
but this could not be the case, as there is
abundant evidence from history that in the
time of our Lord the summit of Tabor was
occupied by a fortified city, and therefore was
not a spot to which Jesus would lead his dis-

ciples with the view of being "apart by themselves." The ruins of the city are still to be
seen on the top of the mountain. Yet the
legend attached to it has always made it resorted to by travellers; and if they cannot
persuade themselves that it is really "the holy
mount," they at least enjoy an extensive view
from the summit, of places familiar and interesting to every reader of Scripture. The mountains of Bashan and Gilead appear in the east
and south-east; in the south are the mountains
of Gilboa, and on the west Carmel. The sight
of these naturally recalled to my mind the
glorious promise made by God, of the restoration and conversion of my dear brethren,—" I
will bring Israel again to his habitation, and
he shall feed on Carmel and Bashan, and his
soul shall be satisfied upon Mount Ephraim and
Gilead. In those days, and in that time, saith
the Lord, the iniquity of Israel shall be sought
for, and there shall be none; and the sins of
Judah, and they shall not be found; for I will
pardon them whom I reserve."*

* Jer. i. 19, 20.

K

Mount Tabor, though not the mount of transfiguration, is not devoid of interesting Scripture recollections. It was here that Deborah and Barak assembled the ten thousand warriors, by whom Sisera was discomfited. Through the plain of Esdraelon, which lies to the west and south-west of Tabor, flows " that ancient river, the river Kishon," celebrated in the triumphal song of Deborah and Barak.*

To the south of Tabor lies Endor, where Saul resorted to consult the woman who had a familiar spirit; and still further south are the mountains of Gilboa, on which that unhappy king and his sons fell, Not far from Endor is the village of Nain, where Christ raised the widow's son.

Feeling much oppressed with thirst from the heat, and fatigue of our ascent, we anxiously sought for some water to refresh us. At length our guide found a very deep well, and with some difficulty contrived, by tying a stone to my leathern bottle, to bring up some water from it. We felt much refreshed by it, and

* Judges, v. 21.

thought it so precious that we were afraid lest a drop should be wasted. I realized the peeuliar appropriateness of the figure so often used in Scripture,—"My soul thirsteth for thee; my flesh longeth for thee in a dry and thirsty land, where no water is."* Would that our longing after the sensible presence of God were a feeling as real and intense as the thirst of the flesh!

After spending about two hours on the summit of Tabor, we again descended, and proceeded on our way to Nazareth, which we reached soon after 4, P.M. The attendants having arrived some hours before us, had pitched our tent in a fig orchard, a pleasant, open place, outside the town.

" The town of Nazareth lies upon the western side of a narrow oblong basin. The houses stand on the lower part of the slope of the western bill, which rises steep and high above them. The name of Nazareth (Arabic, en-Nasirah,) is found in Scripture only in the New Testament. The place is mentioned nei-

* Psalm lxiii. 1.

ther in the Old Testament nor in Josephus,
and was apparently a small and unimportant
village.   'Can there any good thing come out
of Nazareth?" is a question implying anything
but respect; and the appellation of Nazarenes
was in like manner given to the first Christians
in scorn.   Yet to the present day the name for
Christians in Arabic continues to be *en-Nusara*,
that is, Nazarenes."*

"And when they had performed all things
according to the law of the Lord, they returned
into Galilee into their own city Nazareth. And
the Child grew, and waxed strong in spirit,
filled with wisdom."   "And He went down
with them, and came to Nazareth, and was
subject unto them."†

I cannot convey an adequate idea of my
feelings on finding myself at Nazareth ; I could
hardly realize that I was in the very place
where the Saviour of the world, Jesus of Nazareth, lived for thirty years.   I know not how
others feel, but to myself it is much more dif-

* Robinson's Biblical Researches in Palestine, Vol.
III. p. 195-6.   † Luke ii. 39, 40, 51.

ficult to realize that Christ is really man, than that He is really God; it is easier to contemplate Him " exalted at God's right hand to be a prince and Saviour," as one to whom "all power is given in heaven and in earth," than to view Him as being in all respects a brother man. It seems to exceed our belief that He who from all eternity " was with God, and was God," really became a man, and lived upwards of thirty years on this very earth, mingling familiarly with other men, suffering all the evils of poverty, and the trials that arise from intercourse with the ignorant and the depraved; " enduring the contradiction of sinners against himself!"

The Holy Spirit has not seen fit to record much of the life of Jesus during the thirty years He lived previous to His entering on His public career; there is not a single incident of His life given from the time He was twelve years old until he was thirty. But in those psalms where David was carried by the Spirit of God beyond his own feelings and sufferings to those of Christ, we have some glimpses of the exercises of His holy soul, while living in

close contact with sinful men.   John the Baptist prepared for his ministry by a life of
retirement in the wilderness; but He whom it
behoved to be made in all things like unto His
brethren, that He might be a merciful and
faithful High Priest, was trained in the domestic circle; participated in family affections,
and cares, and duties.   He "was subject" to
His mother and her husband; He lived in
social intercourse with His brothers and near
relatives.   They who know the sufferings to
which a Christian is exposed by constant association with those who are not like-minded with
him, may have some perception of the daily
agony of spirit endured by our blessed Lord.
And that His near relatives were not at the
commencement of His ministry like-minded
with Him, we are plainly told.   "For neither
did His brethren believe in Him."   "The
world cannot hate you," said Jesus to them;
"but me it hateth, because I testify of it that
the works thereof are evil."*   Doubtless when
our Lord walked the streets of Nazareth, and

* John vii. 5, 7.

witnessed the various manifestations of the sin
and selfishness of human nature, He fulfilled
that precept of the law,—" Thou shalt in any
wise rebuke thy neighbour, and not suffer sin
upon him."*   And oh, to what suffering must
this have exposed Him!   Those who dwell
apart in their "cieled houses," carefully shun-
ning all intercourse save with the polished and
refined, hating and despising the "vulgar rab-
ble," can but ill imagine the sufferings of Jesus
during His years of privacy and retirement.
The restraints of education tend powerfully to
soften the manners; and the artificial habits of
modern society produce that outward smooth-
ness in social intercourse which prevents the
collision of evil passions, and can even exhibit
an interchange of smiles and civilities between
those whose hearts are burning with hatred
and envy.   But it was not in the polished
circle that Jesus spent His life on earth; the
mean, the coarse, the vicious, "the publicans
and sinners," were those with whom He came
in constant contact.   And did he keep aloof

* Lev. xix. 17.

from them in spirit, though necessitated to mix with them in person? Ah! no, He knew that the meanest among them was still His brother, possessed of some of the kindly affections and better feelings of humanity; He poured forth on them His social sympathy, and sought theirs in return. "I looked for some to take pity, but there was none; and for comforters, but I found none."* "But as for Me, when they were sick, My clothing was sackcloth; I humbled myself with fasting; I bowed down heavily, as one that mourneth for his mother."† But human sympathy and affection were denied Him; the Captain of our salvation was made perfect through sufferings; that His people in all ages might feel that there is no sorrow in which He cannot sympathise with them to the uttermost. His holy soul deeply felt this unkind treatment; He loved His neighbours too well to be able to endure their injuries with cold-hearted indifference, or to repel them with silent contempt. He uttered His complaints to the only ear that

* Psalm lxix. 20.   † Psalm xxxv. 13, 14.

was open to them, even the ear of His Father, and our Father. " For thy sake I have borne reproach, shame hath covered my face. I am become a stranger unto my brethren, and an alien unto my mother's children. I made sackcloth my garment, and I became a proverb to them. They that sit in the gate speak against me; and I was the song of the drunkards."* Cutting reproach and ribald jesting were the response made to the Saviour's yearning for human sympathy!

These, and similar reflections, occurred to me as I walked about by moonlight the evening of our arrival at Nazareth. The next day was Sunday; and here again, though there are three communities professing to be churches of Christ, the Greek, the Romish, and the Maronite, there was none which we could recognise as a church by worshipping with them. A just description of the present spiritual state of Palestine might be given, by exactly reversing the description of its former state, as predicted by Isaiah, and fulfilled in the time of

* Psalm lxix. 7, 8, 11, 12.

our Lord's sojourn on earth. We may say with truth,—"The people that have seen a great light now walk in darkness; those upon whom the light hath shined now dwell in the land of the shadow of death." I remember some years since, when conversing with a Polish Jew, and explaining to him what Christianity is, he said with sincere astonishment,— " If all this be true, why do they not send missionaries from England to convert the Christians in Poland, as well as the Jews? I am sure *you* must know that the Christians there have no more of the religion you have been telling me of than the Jews have." Any Jew in Palestine has a right to put the same question ; and would be quite justified in saying,—" If you call *that* Christianity, I shall cling more closely to Judaism." Those who wish to teach Christianity to the Jews, instead of smoothly commending, must boldly reprove and repudiate the spurious Christianity of the East.

As the morning advanced, the heat of the tent became intolerable ; at half past ten o'clock the thermometer inside the tent was 104, F.

We therefore went into a room in the Latin Convent, where we remained until the cool of the evening. While there we read and considered Luke iv., in which is narrated the commencement of our Lord's ministry. After having taught in the synagogues of Galilee, in such a manner that "there went out a fame of Him through all the region round about." "He came to Nazareth, where He had been brought up ; and as His custom was, He went into the Synagogue on the Sabbath day, and stood up for to read." As He expounded to them the errands of love on which He had come, "to preach the gospel to the poor, to heal the broken-hearted, and preach deliverance to the captives," they "all bore Him witness, and wondered at the gracious words which proceeded out of His mouth." But when He came to rebuke, and to a personal application of His discourse, they "were filled with wrath, and rose up, and thrust Him out of the city, and led Him unto the brow the hill whereon their city was built, that they might cast Him down headlong." Thus, "He came to His own, and His own received Him not." We have no record of His ever again preaching in Nazareth, or even visiting it; as, though it is afterwards mentioned that He returned into " His own country," that is, Lower Galilee, it is evident from Mat. iv. 13, xii. 46—50, and xiii. 1, that both He and His family had moved their abode to one of the towns on the Lake of Tiberias. The men of Nazareth put away from them the word of salvation, and the Lord went to other cities and villages, visiting them no more. And thus it is still. So long as the Gospel is preached in general terms, men of the world listen to it, and even approve it; but when it is pressed home, when it is said, " Thou art the man," they are, like the men of Nazareth, " filled with wrath;" and if they cannot thrust the preacher from them, they remove from him, and seek "smooth things" elsewhere.

In the afternoon we returned to our orchard of fig trees, and I felt indescribable pleasure in looking around me, and thinking that the eyes of our blessed Saviour had rested on the same objects I now beheld, that perhaps He had walked in the very place·where I was now walking. It gave to me a feeling of the reality of His humanity, such as I never had before.

Beneath the church of the Latin Convent is a grotto, in which, it is said, the Virgin Mary was when the Angel appeared to her. The church is from this called the Church of the Annunciation. Over this grotto is said to have stood her house, which has since taken its flight to Loretto. These monkish traditions have seldom any other effect than that of breaking in upon and disturbing one's own sacred associations. Some of them are palpably absurd. The Mount of Precipitation, as they call it, or the spot from whence the men of Nazareth were about to cast down Jesus, instead of being on the " brow of the hill whereon the city is built," is a precipice about two miles distant from Nazareth.

We left Nazareth on the morning of the 15th, and as we rode along I gazed on every object with unabated interest. We had still in view Endor and Nain, Jezreel and Shunam, and the mountains of Gilboa. About noon, we stopped at a well to take some refreshment; there was no pleasant shade to shelter us, but a well of good water is even more indispensable to a traveller in a dry and thirsty land than "the shadow of a great rock," acceptable as this is. Soon after we arrived, a number of women came to draw water; and, as usual, a great deal of quarrelling ensued among them as to who was to get first to draw the water. We had a similar scene of squabbling constantly before our eyes at the well of the Virgin at Nazareth, which was close to the place where our tent was pitched. How many Scripture scenes did this recall to mind! The interview of Moses with the daughters of Reuel, where the same contest seems to have taken place; as well as the more ancient ones of Eliezer with Rebecca, and Jacob with Rachel. I was much struck with the appearance of many of the young women, who, though merely clothed with a coarse wrapper, had several bracelets on their arms, and wore ear-rings and nose-jewels. One of them filled the trough for our horses and mules, but not quite with the grace of Rebecca or Rachel, as she evidently expected a *backshish** for so doing. I could understand Eliezer's test of an amiable and

* A gift.

generous woman, likely to make his master's son happy.

After resting about an hour, we proceeded on our journey. Our ride was far from agreeable, as we met several rough and savage-looking personages, armed with guns and spears. The country is in a very disturbed state; there is a constant warfare going on between the Bedonins and the Arabs. We learned afterwards that there had been a fight that day, in which the former lost ten, and the latter thirty men. They constantly rob and plunder one another, and there seems no law nor government to interfere. In this country one sees more plainly than in any other that the swords are not yet turned into ploughshares, nor the spears into pruning hooks; for every villager one meets is armed, and a shepherd tends his flock, not with a pastoral staff and crook, but with sword and gun.

About five o'clock in the afternoon we arrived at a village called Burka, distant from Samaria about an hour's journey. We could not get any place to pitch our tent free from thorns; this, indeed, was a very common evil;

but here it was worse than usual. We tried to
get in the village a spade or hoe, with which
we might clear the ground, but such imple-
ments were quite unknown to the inhabitants
of Burka, and are so to many others in this
land. It says much for the fertility of the soil ·
(where the ground is arable at all) that they
obtain such crops as they do, since all their
agriculture consists in scratching the surface of
the ground with a wretched plough.

We at length procured an axe, and with it
contrived to clear the floor of our tent a little,
so as to enable us to spread our mats. We
were much annoyed by the people of the village
crowding about our tent, as it required constant watching lest we should have our things
stolen.

Next morning we set out at six o'clock, and
in about an hour we came to the site of ancient
Samaria, the capital of the kingdom of Israel
after the revolt of the ten tribes. It was built
by Omri, the sixth king of Israel. " He bought
the hill Samaria of Shemer for two talents of
silver, and built on the hill, and called the
name of the city which he built after the name

of Shemer, owner of the hill Samaria."* The
scenery here is truly beautiful; it is one of the
very few spots in Palestine to which I could
apply such an epithet.   Many other portions,
I doubt not, were so in their days of cultivation, and will again be so when "the land that
was desolate is become like the garden of
Eden ;"† but in their present waste condition,
they are very unlike all that we are accustomed
to call beautiful in Italy, or any European
country.

"The fine round swelling hill, or almost
mountain of Samaria, stands alone in the midst
of this great basin of some two hours‡ in di-
ameter, surrounded by higher mountains on
every side. .The mountains and the vallies
around are to a great extent arable, and enli-
vened by many villages and the hand of cultivation.   From all these circumstances, the
situation of the ancient Samaria is one of great
beauty."§   " It continued to be the capital of
Israel for two centuries, and until the carrying

* I Kings, xvi. 24.   † Ezek. xxxvi. 35.   ‡ About
six miles.   § Robinson's Biblical Researches in Palestine, vol. iii. 138.

away of the ten tribes by Shalmaneser under
King Hoshea, about 720, B. C. Augustus
('the Roman emperor') bestowed Samaria on
Herod the Great, who ultimately rebuilt the
city with great magnificence and strength, and
gave it the name Sebaste, in honour of Augustus."*

Samaria is associated with several of the miracles of Elijah and Elisha; and its New Testament associations are also interesting.   In
our Lord's time the Holy Land was divided
into four separate regions—Galilee in the
north, Samaria in the middle, Judea in the
south, all these being within, or on the west
side of the Jordan; while the region beyond,
or to the east of Jordan, was called Perœa.
The Samaritans mentioned in the New Testament were the descendants of the mixed multitude placed by the King of Assyria "in the
cities of Samaria, instead of the children of
Israel." The Samaritans had a temple of their
own on Mount Gerizim, and offered sacrifices

* Robinson's Biblical Researches, vol. iii. 147.   The
name Sebaste is the Greek translation of the Latin
epithet or name *Augusta*.

according to the law of Moses; but the Jews refused to acknowledge them as being of the true religion, and had a great enmity against them. As a reproach to our Lord, they said to him,—"Thou art a Samaritan, and hast a devil."*

The Samaritans seem to have formed a sort of middle class between Jews and Gentiles. When our Lord sent forth His twelve apostles, He said,—"Go not into the way of the Gentiles, and into any city of the Samaritans enter ye not; but go rather to the lost sheep of the house of Israel."† And though a Christian church was gathered in Samaria through the preaching of Philip, several years before the conversion of Cornelius and his friends, it is evident these were reckoned the first Gentile converts.

Many are the denunciations in Scripture against Samaria, and they have been fulfilled to the very letter. I cannot illustrate this better than by quoting the interesting account given by the Scotch deputation. "We read

* John viii. 48.   † Mat x. 5, 6.

over the prophecy of Micah (Mich. i. 6,) regarding Samaria as we drew near to it, and conversed together as to its full meaning. We asked Dr. Keith what he understood by the expression, 'I will make Samaria *as an heap of the field.*' He replied, that he supposed the ancient stones of Samaria would be found, not in the form of a ruin, but gathered into heaps in the same manner as they do in clearing a vineyard, or as our farmers at home clear their fields by gathering the stones together. In a little after we found the conjecture to be completely verified. We halted at the eastern end of the hill," and "ascended on foot by a narrow and steep pathway, enclosed by rude dykes, the stones of which are large, and many of them carved, and these are piled rather than built upon one another. Some of them are loose, and ready to fall. Indeed the whole face of this part of the hill suggests the idea that the buildings of the ancient city had been thrown down from the brow of the hill. Ascending to the top, we went round the whole summit, and found marks of the same process everywhere. The people of the country, in order to make room for their fields and gardens, have swept off the old houses, and poured the stones down into the valley ;"* thereby literally fulfilling the latter part of the verse above alluded to,—"I will pour down the stones thereof into the valley."

Besides these remains of the ancient city of Samaria, there are a great many pillars standing, the remnants of a magnificent colonnade, supposed to be of the time of Herod the Great. But the most entire and conspicuous ruin of the place is that of the church of St. John the Baptist, said to be erected over the spot where he was buried. This three-fold character of the ruins was very striking to my mind ; Samaritan, Pagan, and nominally Christian edifices, all involved in one common destruction. And can we say that the last did not deserve its doom as much as the other two ? Nowhere do the absurdities of Popery, or the useless ceremonies of formal Christianity, appear so revolting as in the Holy Land, because there they obviously appear a vain mockery of that

* Narrative of a Mission of Enquiry to the Jews by the Church of Scotland, p. 293-4.

former dispensation, which, when it had served the end for which God appointed it, "was abolished," "for the weakness and unprofitableness thereof." There is scarcely a place in Palestine where you can say to the Jew,— " Behold the desolation of your cities ;" where he cannot point to the ruined church, and say in return,—" What meaneth this?"

There is a modern village called Sebustieh, situated a little way up the hill of Samaria ; its name is a corruption of Sebaste, the name given to Samaria by Herod the Great. The Jews, however, seem to have retained the ancient name, as the city is always called Samaria in the New Testament.

After travelling rather more than two hours farther, we arrived at the town of Nabloos, the Shechem of the Old, and Sychar of the New, Testament. It is a long narrow town, situated at the base of Mount Gerizim, in the valley between that hill and Mount Ebal. These mounts of the blessing and the curse, (Deut. xxvii. 11—13; and Josh. viii. 33, 34.) rise each to the height of about eight hundren feet above the narrow valley that divides them, which is here not above five hundred yards wide. How affecting to look upon Mount Ebal and remember that the curse has come upon Israel to the uttermost! But a time shall yet come when, the veil being taken from their hearts, all the promised blessings shall be theirs. They shall yet be " blessed in the city, and blessed in the field."*

This place is full of Scripture recollections : it is the first spot mentioned in the promised land. After the Lord had said unto Abraham, " Get thee out of thy country, and from thy kindred," this was the first place he came to ;† and here the Lord appeared to him and said, " Unto thy seed will I give this land." Near this Jacob spread his tent on his return from Padan-aram, and dwelt for a time, until the wickedness of his sons in slaying the men of Shechem made a removal desirable ; and the Lord ordered him to Bethel. It was here that all Israel assembled to make Rehoboam king, and that the revolt of the ten tribes took place. It was also one of the cities of refuge, to which

* Deut. xxviii. 3.   † Gen. xii. 6, 7.

the man-slayer might flee from the avenger of blood.

" After the exile, Shechem is mainly known as the chief seat of the people, who thenceforth bore the name of Samaritans. When the Jews returned under Zerubbabel from their exile, and began to build Jerusalem and their temple, the Samaritans also desired to aid them in the work. " Let us build with you, for we seek the Lord as ye do, and we do sacrifice unto him since the days of Esar-haddon."* It was the refusal of the Jews to admit them to this privilege that gave rise to the subsequent hatred between the two races."† It is a remarkable circumstance that to this day there is a small remnant of the Samaritans still living in this place. They only amount to about a hundred and fifty individuals ; but they are still as distinct from Jews and Gentiles as they were in the days of our Saviour. The five books of Moses, or Pentateuch, is the only part of the Bible they receive ; of this they have some very ancient manuscripts, and

* Ezra. iv. 2.
† Robinson's Biblical Researches, vol. iii. 116.

with the exception of a few unimportant verbal differences, their version of the Pentateuch is exactly the same as that of the Jews. This is one of many instances in which the wrath of man has been over-ruled by God to His glory. It is a great proof that the Jewish Scriptures have been handed down without alteration, when this testimony to their faithfulness is borne by a people who have always been at enmity with them. At the first establishment of the Samaritans in Palestine, more than 700 years before Christ, " one of the priests whom they had carried away from Samaria came and dwelt in Bethel, and taught them how they should fear the Lord."* From him they would receive the Pentateuch in use in the kingdom of Israel. Although Jeroboam, the Son of Nebat (whose residence was this very Shechem), introduced idol-worship into the kingdom, and ordained feasts " which he had devised of his own heart," it is evident the knowledge of the true religion had not been entirely rooted out; as may be proved, not

* 2 Kings xvii. 28.

M

only by the instances of Elijah and Elisha, and
the seven thousand who had not bowed the
knee to Baal, but by the existence of several
schools of the prophets at Bethel and elsewhere.*   By the "sons of the prophets"
would the law be carefully preserved; and it
was probably a copy belonging to some of
them that the Samaritans received, as their in-
structor was from Samaria, and not from
Judah, and they never had any friendly intercourse with the Jews.   From the time of Solomon, therefore, we have the five books of
Moses handed down to us entirely independent
of the Jews, and by a people who have always
been at enmity with them.   Even in the present day there is a great shyness between the
Jews and Samaritans; they not only do not
intermarry, nor worship together, but have no
social intercourse.

We only remained a few hours at Nabloos,
being now anxious to arrive at Jerusalem as
soon as possible.   About half an hour after we
left the city we came to Jacob's well.   The

* See 1 Kings xx. 35.

visit to this memorable spot was indeed a spiritual feast to me, calling up, as it did, such
rich stores of meditation, reaching from the
time of Jacob to the days of Jacob's Lord,
" the Angel who redeemed him from all evil."

Jacob was journeying from Padan-aram to
the land of his fathers: he had wrestled with
the Angel of the Covenant and received the
name of Israel, " a prince of God ;" "and he
came to Shalem, a city of Shechem, and
pitched his tent before the city. And he
bought a parcel of a field where he had spread
his tent, at the hand of the children of Hamor, Shechem's father, for an hundred pieces
of money ; and he erected there an altar, and
called it El-elobe-Israel :"* that is, "God, the
God of Israel."

Here, then, I was in the first spot in the
Holy Land that had ever been possessed by
my fathers, as Abraham had owned nothing
but a burying-place therein. When Jacob first
left his father's house, after having enjoyed a
glorious vision at Bethel, " he vowed a vow,

Genesis xxxiii. 18—20.

saying : If God will be with me, and will keep me in this way that I go, and will give me bread to eat, and raiment to put on, so that I come again to my father's house in peace, then shall the Lord be my God, and this stone which I have set for a pillar shall be God's house."* God had fulfilled all his petitions, and brought him again in peace to his father's land ; but instead of hastening to Bethel to perform his vow, he settled down here for some years. How prone are we, in the time of outward prosperity, to forget the vows "which our lips have uttered, and our mouth hath spoken, when we were in trouble!" Jacob had bitterly to repent this sojourn near Shechem ; it probably began in worldly expediency, and it ended in shame and bloodshed. It must have been a time of religious deelension with Jacob when his household had " strange gods among them."† But family affliction in its most trying form, that of family sin, roused him from this state, and God reminded him of his vow. " God said unto

* Gen. xxviii. 20—22. † Gen. xxxv. 2.

Jacob, Arise, go up to Bethel and dwell there, and make there an altar unto God, that appeared unto thee when thou fleddest from the face of Esau thy brother."*

This property Jacob retained, and used as pasturage for his flocks after he was settled in Hebron. When Joseph was sent to inquire after the welfare of his brethren, they had gone "to feed their father's flock in Shechem."† It is to this day one of the few places in Palestine that are well-watered and fertile. "It is difficult," says Robinson, "to account for the fact that a well should have been dug here at all, on a spot in the immediate vicinity of so many natural fountains. I can solve this difficulty only by admitting that this is probably the actual well of the patriarch. The practice of the patriarchs to dig wells wherever they sojourned is well known; and if Jacob's field, as it would seem, was here before the mouth of the valley of Shechem, he might prefer not to be dependent for water on foun-

* Gen. xxxv. 1.   † Ibid. v. 12.

tains which lay up that valley, and were not his own."*

There is a low vaulted chamber built over the mouth of the well, the lower part of which may have been originally the ledge that surrounded it, on which, or on a similar one of an older date, our Lord may have sat to rest when weary with his journey. I cannot express the feeling of vivid reality which the sight of this well gave to the history and the scene connected with it. Jesus "left Judea, and departed again into Galilee: And he must needs go through Samaria,"† which lay directly between Judea and Galilee, unless He had taken a very circuitous road, crossing and recrossing the Jordan. As he sat on the well, faint and weary, "there cometh a woman of Samaria to draw water." All travellers express surprise why a woman of Samaria should come a mile and a half to draw water, when there are fountains close to the town of Sychar. I think there is every reason to suppose she did so as a reli-

* Robinson's Bib. Res. vol. iii. 112.   † John iv. 3, 4.

gions ceremony, similar to that practised by
the Jews in Jerusalem on the great day of the
Feast of Tabernacles. Let it not be supposed
that her being a professor of religion was at all
inconsistent with her leading an immoral life;
in the East to this day the most devout ex-
pressions of piety towards God are often
uttered by persons of vicious character, without
their having an idea that there is any inconsis-
tency between their avowed principles and
their practice. This is a constant source of
complaint among missionaries in Syria.*
When our Lord had told this woman "all
things that ever she did," she perceived He
was a prophet, and immediately sought instruction from Him on the disputed point between Jews and Samaritans as to which was
the holy place, where men ought to worship.
How striking is the reply of our Lord, when
considered in the very place where the fulfil-

* "She was a Druze, and talked most fluently and
piously. Pious language being so universal in this

example than our words upon those around us."—Me-
moir of Mrs. Smith of the Mission in Syria, p. 276,
Boston Edit. 1840.

ment of its prediction is now so manifest,—
" Woman, believe me the hour cometh when
ye shall neither in this mountain, nor yet at
Jerusalem, worship the Father." He next
plainly told her with which of the contending
parties the truth then lay. " Ye worship ye
know not what; we know what we worship,
for salvation is of the Jews." To one of His
brethren according to the flesh, these words,
" We know what we worship," are peculiarly
affecting, our Lord so plainly identifying himself with the Jews. But how important to all
His true disciples of every nation under heaven
is the declaration that follows,—" But the time
cometh, and now is, when the true worshippers shall worship the Father in spirit and in
truth; for the Father seeketh such to worship
Him; God is a spirit, and they that worship
Him must worship Him in spirit and in
truth."* As if he said,—" At present ' salvation is of the Jews;' there is with them,
and their institutions, an arbitrary and official
sanctity, appointed by God Himself; and all

* John iv. 21—24

who would worship aright must be joined with them ; but the hour is at hand when this state of things shall pass away. Now there are 'ordinances of divine service, and a worldly sanctuary,' because 'the way into the holiest of all is not yet made manifest; * now there 'are priests that offer gifts according to the law, who serve unto the example and shadow of heavenly things ;'† but when the 'one sacrifice' has been offered, when the great reality has come, all these shadows shall vanish, official sanctity of place and person shall cease, and nothing shall henceforward be accounted as worship, save the homage of the heart,—the worship of God in spirit and in truth." More than eighteen centuries have elapsed since this declaration, (John iv. 21--24) and yet we find in the Christian church, instead of a universal testimony that it is the Spirit alone that quickeneth, the flesh profiteth nothing, a cleaving to outward rites and ceremonies, as if these were still the appointed channels through which the Spirit is conveyed! A large portion of the pro-

* Heb. ix. 1, 8.   † Heb viii. 4, 5.

fessing Church of Christ seem still in the condition of the Samaritan woman, obliged to go to the well of Jacob to draw water, instead of possessing in themselves "a well of water springing up into everlasting life." If I am still to be dependant on a priest either for the commencement or sustenance of spiritual life, I see little to distinguish the Christian from the Jewish dispensation; if, instead of hereditary priests of a sacred family, chosen by God Himself, I am directed to regard as officially holy, priests made by the will of man, in many cases from mere worldly motives; if I am to have priests without Urim and Thummim, and a temple without a Shechinah, instead of giving me a substance in lieu of a shadow, I am only presented with an empty mockery of a glory that has departed. The Church of Christ may still be edified by *real* gifts, and *real* sanctity; but the ritual and official are mere " beggarly elements," passed away for ever.

The place where Jacob's well is situated is called in the New Testament, " The parcel of ground that Jacob gave to his son Joseph."*

* John iv.

" And the bones of Joseph, which the children of Israel brought up out of Egypt, buried they in Shechem, in a parcel of ground which Jacob bought of the sons of Hamor."* At a short distance from the well is a tomb, said to be built on the spot where Joseph's bones are buried. In the tradition respecting Jacob's well and Joseph's tomb, Jews, Samaritans, Christians, and Mohammedans all agree, and the situation in regard to Sychar corresponds so exactly with the Scripture account, that there is no reason to doubt its correctness. The present name of Sychar, Nabloos, is a corruption of its Roman appellation, Neapolis. I must not omit to mention that one of the American missionaries, some years ago, sounded Jacob's well, and found it seventy-five feet deep, having ten feet of water in it. The Samaritan woman might truly say " the well is deep."

After viewing this interesting spot we proceeded on our journey. The travelling on this day was rendered very uncomfortable by the

* Joshua xxiv. 32.

scarcity of water. My friend M. having lost his leathern bottle, we had only mine to depend upon; and the water it contained was soon spent. I thought of poor Hagar when suffering a similar privation. At length we came to a little pool of water supplied by a feeble spring. It was full of insects. One of the Arab guards, who had accompanied us from Nazareth, seeing me hesitate to drink it, kindly pulled down his shirt sleeve over his wrist, and offered it to me as a filter! I need hardly say I declined his obliging offer.

We pitched our tent this evening at a village called Lubbon, the ancient Lebonah, mentioned in Judges xxi. 19. Like other Arab villages, it consists merely of a few huts built of mud; but the situation is fine, being on the acclivity of one of those terraced hills that are frequently met with in Palestine. With great labour the sides of the hills have been cut into flat terraces, or ledges of rock, to which soil must have been artificially conveyed. On these terraces the vines were cultivated. This explains the allusion of the Psalmist in speaking of Israel as a vine brought out of Egypt : " The hills were

covered with the shadow of it." From the
terraces of this, and of some of the other bills,
the soil has been completely washed away, and
nothing but the bare rock remains. But the
sure word of prophecy has said to the daughter
of Israel : " Thou shalt yet plant vines upon
the mountains of Samaria."*

About three miles from Lubban, " on the
east side of the highway that goeth up from
Bethel to Shechem, and on the south of Lebonah,"† is the site of the ancient Shiloh, where
the ark and tabernacle were from the time of
Joshua, until that of Eli. Surely if any thing
could consecrate a portion of this accursed
earth, the visible manifestation of Jehovah's
presence for so many years must have done
so ; but what is the fact? When God "for-
sook the tabernacle of Shiloh," the place
became common and unclean. Even in the
days of type and shadow, there was no holiness
conceived to remain after God had departed.

Soon after we had pitched our tent, we saw
a number of the villagers running out, armed

* Jer. xxxi. 5.   † Judges xxi. 19.

with guns and swords. We learned that the inhabitants of a neighbouring village had stolen away some of their cattle ; and they were going forth to endeavour to recover them. In about an hour after, they returned in triumph, shouting with all their might. Happily, the victory was a bloodless one ; at the firing of the first gun, the prey was abandoned, and the robbers fled. This gave us a melancholy picture of the state of the people ; rapine and petty warfare without, and the utter absence of every thing like domestic comfort at home. Who can sufficiently estimate the blessings of civilisation! How constantly does it follow, how rarely does it precede, a knowledge of true religion ; which, like its divine author, sheds its temporal blessings on the just and the unjust; those who refuse to admit its light within them still enjoying the advantages derived from its shining around them.

Next morning we rose very early to set out on our journey to Jerusalem. I felt a feverish restlessness and anxiety to reach that city, which had been associated in my mind from childhood, with all that is sacred and venerable;

and I often said within myself as we rode
along : "Is it possible that this very day my
feet shall stand within the gates of Jerusalem?"

Our route lay for some time through a fertile
plain which had some appearance of cultivation;
there being several fields of millet in it. But
the farther we advanced on our journey the
more barren and desolate the country became.
My mind was alternately occupied with two
very different pictures. At one time I thought
of the days when all the male population of
Israel went up " three times in a year" to Jerusalem ; " whither the tribes go up, the tribes
of the Lord, unto the testimony of Israel, to
give thanks unto the name of the Lord."*
In all probability six of the tribes, whose pos-
sessions lay northward of where I then was,
travelled by this very road ; the party increasing at every stage of their journey ; "company
by company," until they all " appeared before
God in Zion."†   As I thought of this goodly
assembly, all animated by one spirit, and intent
on one common object, receiving each new

* Psa. cxxii. 4.   † Psa. lxxxiv. 7.

accession of brethren with friendly greetings, and beguiling the way with social converse, the melancholy contrast presented by the present state of the country forcibly recalled the opposite picture, as delineated in the writings of the prophets.   Nay, I should not say the picture was recalled; the very reality was itself before me.   "The highways" are indeed "desolate" and "lie waste;" instead of being trodden by a joyous company of Israel's sons, a few strangers from distant lands come to behold the judgments of the Lord, and to "say, when they see the plagues of that land, —that it is not sown nor beareth, nor any grass groweth therein:—Wherefore hath the Lord done thus in this land? What meaneth the heat of this great anger?" *

The marks of the curse are indeed upon the land.   Sometimes a green spot will be seen at a distance, giving the idea of fertility; but when approached, it is found to bear only the tokens of the original denunciation,—thorns and briers.

We rode on hour after hour, amid increasing

* Deut. xxix. 23, 24.

desolation. The latter part of the way lies over a succession of mountainous ridges, where there is no regular road, but the horses clamber up the best way they can, sometimes over smooth slabs of stone, and sometimes through heaps of loose stones. My impatience to see the holy city increased every hour. As we climbed up each ridge, I expected that, from its summit, I should behold Jerusalem; but I was doomed to many disappointments; as summit after summit only gave to view another range of hills to be surmounted. It forcibly reminded me of the journey to the Heavenly Jerusalem, which is a steep and difficult path, presenting one mountain after another to be overcome; but we know that at last we shall reach the City of God; and should not the certainty of this reconcile us to all the difficulties of the way? While, on this tedious journey, I was made fully. to understand the comparison of the Psalmist: "As the mountains are round about Jerusalem, so the Lord is round about his people from henceforth even for ever."*

* Psa. cxxv. 2.

N 2

At length the long-expected moment arrived :
about noon we reached the summit of the hill
Scopus, and all at once Jerusalem burst upon
my view.   The feelings of such a moment
cannot be described; they can only be faintly
imagined by those who have not experienced
them.   Every Christian traveller speaks of the
feeling as overpowering : what, then, was it to
me, as at once a Christian and a Jew!   The
scene of the world's redemption,—the metro-
polis of the country of my fathers, — "the
City of the Great King !"   I could, in some
faint measure, realise the feelings of my blessed
Lord and Master, when " He beheld the city,
and wept over it."

But here, as every where else in the Holy
Land, you are indebted to association alone.
That which actually meets your view is a comparatively modern eastern city; her bulwarks
and her palaces are those of the false prophet.
The Lord has abhorred IIis sanctuary ; He
has given it to be "trodden down of the Gentiles, until the times of the Gentiles be fulfilled." *   How near this may be who can tell !

* Luke xxi. 24.

We went first to the Damascus gate, but were not admitted; we then went round to the Jaffa gate; and by it I entered the Holy City. My feet stood " within the gates of Jerusalem;" a pilgrim and a stranger I entered the city of my fathers, " Jerusalem which is in bondage with her children ;"* yet, through the great mercy of God, a citizen of "the Jerusalem which is above."

My first object of inquiry was after letters from my real home,—my distant home in my adopted country. Not having heard of my family for several weeks, I was truly rejoiced to find letters awaiting me here; and fully realised the scripture truth; "As cold waters to a thirsty soul, so is good news from a far country."†

I had soon the pleasure of meeting with two brethren in Christ, and according to the flesh, Bishop Alexander, and Mr. Calman; from both of whom, as well as from the American missionaries, I received the most Christian and friendly attentions during my stay in Jerusalem.

* Gal. iv. 25. † Prov. xxv. 25.

I had also the pleasure of renewing my acquaintance with another Jewish brother, the
Rev. Mr. Ewald. I feel it right especially to
bear testimony to the kindness of Bishop.
Alexander; opposed as we are in our views of
many things that relate to the Church of
Christ, and differing from him, as I do, on the
subject of the mission at Jerusalem, which
difference I never for a moment concealed from
him, he continued from first to last to treat me
with the utmost courtesy and hospitality.

We spent the day after our arrival in visiting, under the guidance of Mr. Calman, the
various remarkable localities immediately round
the city, as we wished first to take a general
view, and return afterwards to those spots that
most deeply interested us. Instead of detail-
ing the events of each day, it will be more
interesting to my readers to give them a brief
account of the city, and the chief places of
interest in and around it.

" Jerusalem lies near the summit of a broad
mountain ridge. All around are higher hills;
on the east, the Mount of Olives; on the
south, the Hill of Evil Counsel, so called, rising

directly from the Vale of Hinnom ; on the west the ground rises gently to the borders of the Great Wady, while on the north a bend of the ridge connected with the Mount of Olives bounds the prospect at the distance of more than a mile."* The present city is surrounded by a wall, and entered by four gates. Dr. Robinson made a careful measurement of the wall, and found it to be two and a half miles round.

Jerusalem is first mentioned in connexion with Melchizedek, who was king of Salem. That this is the same place which was afterwards called Jerusalem is evident, from Psalm lxxvi. 2. "In Salem also is his tabernacle, and his dwelling-place in Zion." We next hear of it under the name of Jebusi, or the city of the Jebusites, whom the children of Benjamin could not drive out, but who continued to dwell in this their fortified city until the time of David. When David was anointed king over all Israel, he went up to this stronghold to extirpate the last of the heathens from

* Robinson's Biblical Researches, i. 382.

the land of Israel; they trusted in the lame and blind idols which they set on the wall as a defence; but David overcame them, and made this city the capital of his kingdom. It was builded "as a city in which *men* were to be united together;" it was to be a centre of unity to the whole nation of Israel; "whither the tribes go up, the tribes of the Lord, unto the testimony of Israel."* Three times in a year was it filled with "the many thousands of Israel" who went to the "city of their solemnities" to keep the appointed feasts. From the sacred bond of union which Jerusalem thus formed, it was regarded with holy veneration; and is spoken of as the type or personification of the church. "If I forget thee, O Jerusalem, let my right hand forget her cunning:"† "Pray for the peace of Jerusalem; they shall prosper that love thee."‡

It was in the days of Solomon that the city was in the height of its glory; when he "made silver in Jerusalem as stones, and cedar trees as the sycamore trees;"§ when "Judah

* Psalm cxxii. 3, 4.   † Psalm cxxxvii. 5.
‡ Psalm cxxii. 6.   § 2 Chronicles ix. 27.

and Israel were many, as the sand which is by
the sea in multitude;" and "dwelt safely,
every man under his vine, and under his fig-
tree."*

When thinking of its former magnificence,
and viewing it now, how appropriate do the
words of Jeremiah appear! "How doth the
city sit solitary, that was full of people! How
is she become as a widow! She that was great
among the nations, and princess among the
provinces, how is she become tributary!"
"The ways of Zion do mourn, because none
come to the solemn feasts."† The word of
the Lord went forth against Jerusalem; that
word which is "a fire, and a hammer that
breaketh the rock in pieces." He said by the
prophet Micah that "Jerusalem shall become
heaps;"‡ and it has been literally fulfilled.
The modern city is built on the heaps of rub-
bish accumulated by the ruins of ancient buildings. So great are these heaps, that in digging
for the foundation of a house, they have to go
to an immense depth before they can get to

* 1 Kings iv. 20, 25. † Lament. i. 1, 4.
‡ Mic. iii. 12.

the solid rock.   On this account a great many
of the present houses are built on arches.
The glory and magnificence of Jerusalem are
gone; she is in bondage, as well as her children.   The jealousy of her Turkish possessors
is ever on the watch, lest anything should seem
to interfere with their despotic sway ; and any
material change in her condition, while they
continue to have the rule, appears impossible.

That which naturally comes to be described,
after the city, is Mount Zion; the whole of
which was anciently inclosed within the wall of
the city, and about one half of which is within
the modern city wall. " David took the stronghold of Zion, the same is the city of David;
so David dwelt in the fort, and called it the
city of David."*   This continued the royal
residence, and became also the burial place of
the kings; but that which gave it a sacred
character, and made it afterwards, like Jerusalem, used to signify the church and nation of
Israel, was the ark of God being placed there
by David.   When we consider that the ark

---

* 1 Samuel, v. 7, 9.

was made by the express command of God,
and that He gave the most minute directions
respecting it, we cannot but wonder at the entire oblivion into which it seems to have fallen
for so long a period. For upwards of ninety
years, that is from the death of Eli, until
David was king over all Israel, the ark appears
to have been in a state of disuse. We hear
once, it is true, of Saul calling for it;* but
David says expressly, when about to take it to
Mount Zion, "Let us bring again the ark of
our God to us; for we inquired not at it in
the days of Saul."† It was probably to teach
Israel again to honour it, as the visible symbol
of His presence, that God saw fit to cut off
Uzzah for his rashness in touching it. This
judgment seems to have reminded David that
the ark was not to be put upon "a new cart,"
after the fashion of the Philistines, but borne
upon the shoulders of the Levites.

"And David made him houses in the city
of David, and prepared a place for the ark of
God, and pitched for it a tent. Then David

* 1 Sam. xiv. 18.   † 1 Chron. xiii. 3.

said : " None ought to carry the ark of God
but the Levites ; for them hath God chosen to
carry the ark of God." *   David and all Israel
brought up the ark with shouting and great
joy, " and set it in his place, in the midst of
the tabernacle that David had pitched for it."†
From this time until the building of the
temple, to which the ark was removed, Zion
was the holy place, or sanctuary of the Lord ;
and the name continued ever after to be used
by prophets and holy men, to designate the
whole of Jerusalem, including the temple. " I
am the Lord your God dwelling in Zion, My
holy mountain."‡   " Is not the Lord in
Zion ?" §

What now remains of the glory of Mount
Zion ?   Nothing.   Its regal splendour, its
hallowed sacredness, are gone : " Therefore
shall Zion for your sake be plowed as a field;"
was the word of the inspired prophet to " the
heads of the house of Jacob, and princes of
the house of Israel ;" ‖ and there is now a field
of barley growing on Zion, as a testimony that

* 1 Chron. xv. 1, 2.   † 2 Samuel, vi. 17.
‡ Joel iii. 17.   § Jer. viii. 19.   ‖ Mic. iii. 9, 12

the word of the Lord standeth sure. Where
now are her bulwarks and her palaces, which
the Psalmist pointed out to the consideration
of the faithful? They are swept away with
the besom of destruction.

Mount Zion is separated by a narrow valley
from mount Moriah, a locality full of interesting associations. Here the father of the faithful was put to the trying test of offering up his
well-beloved son. On this mount, in dutiful
submission to his Heavenly and his earthly
father, he lay bound, from whom afterwards
proceeded the many thousands of Israel.
When Jerusalem was visited with pestilence,
as a punishment for the sin of David in num-
bering the people, it was on this mount the
destroying angel showed himself. It was at
that time the property of one of the original
inhabitants of Jerusalem, Arauneh, or Oruan,
the Jebusite. "And the angel of the Lord
stood by the threshing-floor of Oruan the Jebusite. And David lifted up his eyes, and
saw the angel of the Lord stand between the
earth and the heaven, having a drawn
sword in his hand, stretched out over Jeru-

salem." *   David was commanded to erect
here an altar unto the Lord, and this he fixed
upon as the place whereon the temple should
be built. "Then David said, This is the house
of the Lord God, and this is the altar of the
burnt offering for Israel." †   And here, in due
time, was the magnificent temple reared up by
Solomon, the peaceful prince, the successor of
Melchizedek, "king of Salem, which is king
of peace," ‡ and the type of that "Prince of
Peace," who shall "reign over the house of
Jacob for ever." §

The temple of Solomon, with its courts, occupied the whole summit of Mount Moriah.
But though it was "exceeding magnifical, of
fame and of glory throughout all countries,"‖ it
was not this outward splendour that constituted
the glory of the temple; it was the shechinah,
the abiding presence of the Lord, that was
"the glory in the midst of it."   When the
building was completed, and Solomon had
invoked the presence of the Lord, He condescended to take possession of the habitation

* 1 Chron. xxi. 15, 16.   † Ibid xxi. 1.
‡ Heb. vii. 2.   § Luke 1. 33.   ‖ 1 Chron. xxii. 5.

prepared for him: "Now when Solomon had made an end of praying, the fire came down from heaven, and consumed the burnt offering and the sacrifices; and the glory of the Lord filled the house;" * even as it had before filled the tabernacle in the wilderness.† Here was the true church pointed out with sufficient clearness; to separate from this was indeed schism. This visible manifestation of God's presence continued until the commencement of the captivity. In the visions of Ezekiel, we have a detailed account of the departure of the glory of the Lord from the temple. While a captive by the river Chebar, he was carried "in the visions of God to Jerusalem, to the door of the inner gate—and behold, the glory of the God of Israel was there: Then said he unto me,—son of man, seest thou what they do, even the great abominations that the house of Israel committeth here, that I should go far off from my sanctuary?" ‡ In the following part of the vision we are told that "the glory of the

* 2 Chron. vii. 1.   † Exod. xl. 34.
‡ Ezek. viii. 3, 6.

o 2

Lord went up from the cherub and stood over the threshold of the house;" * the glory then removes to "the east gate of the Lord's house;" † and finally "the glory of the Lord went up from the midst of the city, and stood upon the mountain which is on the east side of the city;" ‡ that is, the Mount of Olives.

When speaking of these localities, in connexion with this vision of the departure of the shechinah, I cannot resist directing my reader's attention to another remarkable vision of the same prophet yet to be fulfilled. The latter portion of Ezekiel's prophecy is occupied with the subject of the future glory of Israel; in which, doubtless, "there are many things hard to be understood;" but this much is very plain, that the things therein predicted did not come to pass at the return from Babylon. Respecting the "house" which occupies such a prominent part in that vision, I offer no opinion; that to which I now wish to direct attention is, the return of the glory of God, whose departure we have just seen so minutely

---

* Ezek. x 4.   † Ibid. 19.   ‡ Ibid. xi. 23.

described. "Afterwards he brought me to
the gate, even the gate that looketh toward
the east ; and behold the glory of the God
of Israel came from the way of the east ; and
his voice was like a nŏise of many waters, and
the earth shined with his glory ;— and the
glory of the Lord came into the house by the
way of the gate whose prospect is towards the
east ;—and behold, the glory of the Lord filled
the house. And he said unto me : Son of man,
the place of my throne, and the place of thĕ
soles of my feet, where I will dwell in the
midst of the children of Israel for ever." *
Compare this with the following Scriptures :
"My tabernacle also shall be with them ; yea,
I will be their God, and they shall be my
people. And the heathen shall know that I
the Lord do sanctify Israel, when my sanctuary
shall be in the midst of them for ever more." †
"And his feet shall stand in that day upon the
Mount of Olives, which is before Jerusalem on
the east. And the Lord shall be king over all
the earth ; in that day shall there be one Lord,

* Ezek. xliii. 1—7.   † lbid. xxxvii. 27, 28.

and his name one." *   "And I heard a great
voice out of heaven saying, Behold the tabernacle of God is with men, and he will dwell
with them." †   These Scriptures I leave without note or comment, to the consideration of
the Christian reader.

We have seen that Zion is plowed as a field,
and Jerusalem has become heaps ; the last denunciation uttered by the prophet Micah has
also been fulfilled, that " the mountain of the
house," should become " as the high places of
a forest."   This latter expression signifies the
places where the worship of a false religion
was carried on ; the " high places " of the heathen, in the prophet's days, being always in a
wood or grove.   This, also, has been fulfilled
to the very letter.   The mosque of Omar, the
sanctuary of the False Prophet, occupies the
place where the temple of the Lord once stood ;
and, as if to fulfil the prophecy more minutely,
the Mohammedans have planted around it
cypress and orange trees ; so that, looking at it
from a distance, it indeed appears "like the
high places of a wood" or forest.

* Zech. xiv. 4, 9.   † Rev. xxi. 3.

It may be instructive to inquire why God has thus permitted that which He has Himself called "My holy mountain" to be defiled; "What meaneth the heat of this great anger?" He has condescended to answer this question very plainly. Before pronouncing the denunciation already so often alluded to, He gives the reason of it: "They build up Zion with blood, and Jerusalem with iniquity. The heads thereof judge for reward, and the priests thereof teach for hire, and the prophets thereof divine for money: yet will they lean upon the Lord and say, Is not the Lord among us? None evil can come upon us. Therefore shall Zion, for your sake, be plowed as a field, and Jerusalem shall become heaps, and the mountain of the house as the high places of the forest." *

The judgments upon Jerusalem afford an example of what is common to many prophetic intimations. The predicted consummation was viewed by the prophet as a great whole; and he simply announced its ultimate condition as

* Micah iii. 10—12.

one great event, without giving any hint that it was produced by successive events, occurring at different times. The objection so often made to a first and second fulfilment of the same prophecy ought to be silenced at once by what we know has actually taken place with regard to Jerusalem. Its desolation is always spoken of in the prophets as one event; yet it has had two distinct fulfilments, at a distance of more than six hundred years from each other. The immediate cause of its destruction by Nebuchadnezzar, is declared by God himself to have been the idolatry and bloodshed of Manasseh. In reference to that overthrow, the Lord says: "I will wipe Jerusalem as a man wipeth a dish, wiping it and turning it upside down."* Those who prayed "for the peace of Jerusalem" were comforted by predictions of her future restoration. It was said to Jerusalem— "Thou shalt be built, and to the temple, thy foundation shall be laid."† Jerusalem and the temple were rebuilt and beautified. Who that saw this restoration would have surmised that

* 2 Kings xxi. 13.   † Isaiah xliv. 28.

a second destruction more complete, and a second desolation more protracted, yet awaited
both? My limits prevent me from pursuing
this subject; I merely throw out this hint to
the diligent student of the word of God, that
the successive fulfilments of the same prophecy,
and the announcement, in one prophecy, of two
events as simultaneous, or closely following
each other, which in reality are separated by a
long period, is the true key to many of the
prophetic scriptures. Could any one discover
in the prediction uttered by John the Baptist,
that the fulfilment of the first part was just at
hand, and that of the latter part many centuries distant? Between the event recorded in
v. 11 of Mat. iii. and those events recorded
in v. 12, the whole of the present dispensation
intervenes.

To return to the destruction of Jerusalem, it
is worthy of remark, that though idolatry was
one great cause of its destruction by the Baby-
lonians, the Jews were generally free from this
sin after the captivity. Nor was there any.

gion. In our Saviour's time, the ordinances

seem to have been rigidly observed. Does He give any countenance to the notion, so frequently brought forward in the present day, that where the form is, we are bound to believe the spirit of God and His blessing are there also? Did He tell His disciples to believe that purity dwelt in a whited sepulchre, or that they must receive a wolf in sheep's clothing as one of the true flock? No; the "spirit of Christ," whether uttered by Himself or by the mouth of the prophet,* spoke the same thing. By Isaiah, He said of the ordinances appointed by His own command, " Incense is an abomination to Me ; the new moons and sabbaths, the calling of assemblies, I cannot away with ; it is iniquity, even the solemn meeting."† By

the ungodliness of the rulers and teachers of the Jewish nation was the cause why Zion should be plowed as a field ; and He Himself said, " Woe unto you, Scribes and Pharisees, hypocrites, for ye make clean the outside of the cup and of the platter, but within they are full

* 1 Peter i. 11.   † Isaiah i. 13.

therefore ye shall receive the greater damnation." *   •

I have dwelt at some length on this subject, because it appears to me one of great importance. Is it not awful that the children of God should appear to attach some holiness to that which they know to be unholy,—which they know God sees to be unholy ? Are there now no religious services that are an abomination to Him ; no " solemn meetings " that He cannot away with ? " Woe unto them that call evil good."

Although, according to our Saviour's prediction, not one stone of the temple is left upon another, there is every reason to believe that the foundations, and some of the lower part of the wall that now encloses the Mosque of Omar, are remains of the ancient wall that enclosed the area where the Temple stood. In one part there is distinctly seen, springing out from the wall, the commencement of an arch

* Matt. xxiii. 25, 14.

formed of very large stones, which has evidently belonged to the bridge that, according to Josephus, connected Mount Zion with Mount Moriah.   At another portion of the old wall the Jews assemble to mourn over the desolation of their city and temple.   After the revolt of the Jews under Adrian, they were. not allowed to approach the Holy City ; " and it was not till the age of Constantine that they were permitted to approach so as to behold Jerusalem from the neighbouring hills.   At length they were allowed to enter the city once a year, on the day on which it was taken by Titus, in order to wail over the ruins of the temple." *

One Friday afternoon Mr. Calman took M. and me to the Jew's place of wailing.   After going along a narrow lane, we came to a small open space, one side of which was bounded by the wall that surrounds the area of the great mosque.   The lower part of this wall is evidently very ancient ; and there is historical evidence that, as far back as the twelfth cen-

* Robinson's Bib. Researches, i. 350.

tury, the Jews regarded it as having belonged
to the court of the ancient temple.

The scene that here presented itself was one
of the most striking I beheld in Jerusalem.
About thirty men, and half as many women,
were assembled together, all without shoes,
the ground whereon they trod being in their
estimation holy.   Some were seated on the
gound reading, some were praying, and others
kissing the wall.   I entered into conversation
with some of the Polish and German Jews,
and inquired what they were reading.   Several
were reading portions of the Psalms; others
the Lamentations of Jeremiah; and one venerable looking old man was reading the account
of Solomon's dedication of the Temple, recorded in 1st Kings, viii.   Who could not sympathise with him in contemplating the constrast
between the glorious scene therein described
and the present desolation of the city and
temple?   Nothing could give a more vivid picture of the humiliation of Israel than these
poor Jews, strangers and outcasts in what used
to be their own city.   " The Lord hath cast

he hath given up into the hand of the enemy
the walls of her palaces."*   "The precious
sons of Zion, comparable to fine gold, how are
they esteemed as earthen pitchers, the work of
the hands of the potter !"†   The sons of Zion,
instead of being objects of interest and pity,
are exposed to the contempt and hatred, not
only of the Mohammedan possessors of their
city, but of the professors of false Christianity
who dwell in it.   I cannot describe the vividness of truth with which the words came home
to me, as I listened to one of my poor brethren
reading the 12th verse of the 1st chapter of
Lamentations,—" Is it nothing to you, all ye
that pass by?   Behold and see if there be any
sorrow like unto my sorrow, which is done
unto me, wherewith the Lord hath afflicted me
in the day of his fierce anger."

We went from this spot to examine more
minutely the fragment of the arch, that interesting relic which so clearly demonstrates the
antiquity of the portion of the wall to which
it belongs, and which is a strong presumptive

* Lament. ii. 7.   † Ibid. iv. 2.

evidence that those parts of the walls that are of similar architecture are equally ancient. M. measured three of the stones that compose this fragment, and found them respectively 21, 23, and 25 feet in length. The distance from this point to the precipitous rock of Zion, on the other side of the valley, was measured by Dr. Robinson, and found to be 350 feet, which was probably the length of the bridge that united the two mounts together : joining the royal residence to the house of God. While standing in the valley between these renowned eminences, and examining the remnant of the bridge that united them, it was interesting to remember that Moriah belonged to the tribe of Benjamin, and Zion to Judah. These two brethren have always been peculiarly united. "Send the lad with me," said Judah to his father ; "I will be surety for him."* When the ten tribes revolted from the house of David these two remained loyal : and to this day the descendants of these two brethren continue united in suffering, wandering together over the wide world, without a country or a home.

* Gen. xliii. 8, 9.

At the other end of the same valley is the pool of Siloam, a reservoir for water, surrounded by ancient walls of hewn stone. It was in this pool our Lord desired the blind man to wash after He had anointed his eyes with clay. The water that supplies the pool comes from a fountain, or perhaps it may rather be called another pool, nearly a quarter of a mile distant, a channel being cut through the hill from the one to the other. It has been conjectured, and there is great reason for the supposition, that the upper pool (which is now called the Fountain of the Virgin) is itself supplied by a spring that rises in Mount Moriah, immediately under the site of the Temple. There is a spring or fountain directly under the mosque of Omar, of the water of which Dr. Robinson drank, and found it had the same peculiar taste he had remarked in the water of Siloam. This reminds one of the vision of Ezekiel, in which he saw waters proceeding " from under the right side of the house at the south side of the altar;"* and

* Ezek. xlvii. 1.

of the prophetic declaration of Joel respecting
the latter days, that then "a fountain shall
come forth of the house of the Lord."*

"Jesus went forth with his disciples over
the brook Cedron, where was a garden. And
Judas knew the place, for Jesus oftimes resorted thither with his disciples."† The brook
Cedron, or Kidron, is now only a dry channel,
through which no stream flows, except during
the heavy rains of winter; but on crossing it,
near the north-east corner of the city, you
come to a plat of ground, enclosed with a
stone wall, which has long been pointed out as
the Garden of Gethsemane; and as the situation corresponds to the place described in the
Gospel narrative, being near the Mount of
Olives, there is little reason to doubt that in or
near this spot the mysterious agony of our
blessed Lord, when he "offered up prayers
and supplications with strong crying and tears
unto him that was able to save him from
death,"‡ took place. In this enclosure are
eight very old olive trees. I felt this a solemn

* Joel iii. 18.   † John xviii. 1, 2.   ‡ Heb. v. 7.

spot; it was impossible to visit it, for the first
time at least, without a lively recollection of
Him who " poured out his soul unto death.'"
I felt how natural to the human mind is the
worship of the visible,—the love of relics.   I
could not resist pulling many twigs of those
ancient olive trees.   It is easy to understand
how, from the time of Peter unto the present
day, men should be disposed to say, when
deeply impressed in a particular spot, " let us
build a tabernacle" here ; but even if expe-
ricuce had not shown the futility of such attempts to perpetuate the impression, I believe
the principle is in itself wrong, as tending to
encourage a low estimate of the degree in
which God's presence may be now enjoyed.
If we really believe that where two or three
are gathered together in Christ's name, He is
there in the midst of them, actually, though
invisibly, present, we ought to feel that to us
the place where He is now present in spirit is
more holy than the place where He was in
person many hundred years ago ; and thus the
upper room, the open field, or our own private
chamber, where God condescends to meet with

us, should be to us "none other than the house of God and the gate of heaven." I firmly believe, that if we seek to affect the mind by the aid of architecture, painting, or music, the impression produced by these adjuncts is just so much subtracted from the worship of the unseen Jehovah. If the outward eye is taken up with material splendour, or forms of external beauty, the mind's eye sees but little of " Him who is invisible ;" the ear that is entranced with the melody of sweet sounds, listens not to the "still small voice" by which the Lord makes his presence known.

Gethsemane is situated near the base of the Mount of Olives, lying a little to the right of the path which leads to the top of the Mount. This mount might almost be called the home of Jesus when he was in Jerusalem : " In the day time he was teaching in the temple ; and at night he went out and abode in the mount that is called the Mount of Olives ;"* yea, when " every man went into his own house, Jesus went unto the Mount of Olives;"† while

* Luke xxi. 37. † John vii. 53 ; viii. 1.

the foxes have holes, and the birds of the air have nests, the Son of man had not where to lay His head.

After walking for about half an hour up a rather steep ascent, we came to the highest summit of the mount. From this there is an extensive view, it being the highest point in the immediate vicinity of Jerusalem. The Dead Sea is distinctly seen, and the valley of the Jordan, which may be traced out by the narrow strip of verdure which distinguishes its banks from the more " dry and barren land" around.

How many associations crowd into the mind on this mount ? When David went forth from Jerusalem, on the rebellion of his son Absalom, he "went up by the ascent of Mount Olivet, and wept as he went up, and had his head covered, and he went barefoot."* While in this state of humiliation, did not the Holy Spirit lead the royal prophet beyond his own sufferings, to those of his Son and his Lord, who afterwards spent so many nights on this

* 2 Samuel xv. 30.

same spot, pouring out His soul in agony for the sins of men? Who knows how many of those psalms, in which are blended the utter-anecs of the feeble and sinful David, and the utterances of Him who, "though He knew no sin," was "made sin for us," were sug-gested to the mind of the Psalmist, as he walked, weeping and barefoot, up this mount!

It was here that Jesus sat with his disciples, when He delivered to them the prophetic an-nouncement of the destruction of Jerusalem, and of the events that characterise "the great and terrible day of the Lord," of which the judgments on Jerusalem were a type.

A very ancient tradition makes the Mount of Olives the scene of the ascension; but it is expressly said in Scripture that Jesus "led them out as far as Bethany;" which is about half a mile beyond it, on the road from Jeru-salem to Jericho. In Acts i. 12, it is true, we are told that the disciples "returned unto Jerusalem from the mount called Olivet;" but this involves no contradiction. The nearest road from Bethany to Jerusalem is directly across the Mount of Olives; and what more

natural than that, after having parted from
their beloved Master, they should linger for a
while in the place where they had so often
taken sweet counsel with Him? The men "in
white apparel" had said to them, "This same
Jesus which is taken up from you into heaven,
shall so come in like manner as ye have seen
him go into heaven;"* and Zechariah had
prophecied in connexion with the final affliction of Jerusalem, that "His feet shall stand
in that day upon the Mount of Olives." May
we not suppose that on coming to the spot
where, a few weeks before Jesus had told them
"the signs of his coming, and of the end of
the world," that they tarried for a time, before
returning to the bustle of the city, to "comfort
one another" with anticipations of their Lord's
return; that here "they worshipped him,"
and were thus enabled to "return to Jerusalem
with great joy?"†

Bethany is a mean village, containing about
twenty families; but is deeply interesting from
having been the abode of those whom Jesus

* Acts i. 11.   † Luke xxiv. 52.

loved ; the place to which He so often resorted to enjoy the sympathy and friendship of a pious family, after having "endured the contradiction of sinners against himself." How interesting to contemplate the holy, yet real humanity of Christ! That He who was " Lord of all " should condescend to bestow a special love on some of His disciples! Possibly it was to take a last farewell of this family, that He "led them out as far as Bethany" before leaving the earth.

The pretended house and tomb of Lazarus, together with the house of Simon the Leper, are shown at Bethany ; but these, and all similar traditions, are generally fictions of the fourth century, or later ; and in many cases are not merely doubtful, but directly opposed to the scriptural account. After the professed conversion of the Emperor Constantine to Christianity, pilgrimages to the Holy City became the fashion of the day ; his mother Helena went thither at the age of eighty ; and caused churches to be built at Bethlehem and the Mount of Olives, to commemorate the nativity and the ascension. This continued the fashion of the religious world for many succeeding centuries; and each century presented some new discovery of a venerated locality, and the erection of a church or monastery on the supposed site of a memorable place or scene of a remarkable event. In due time all these discoveries came to be ascribed to Helena; and although in the writings of her contemporaries she is only said to have built the two churches above mentioned, " in the fourteenth century not less than thirty churches were ascribed to her within the limits of Palestine."* These "lying vanities" met us at every stage of our journey in the Holy Land; but so far from thinking any of them worthy of notice, I conceive they would only be to my readers, as they were to myself, an impertinent annoyance, destroying hallowed associations, and tending to make one view with suspicion all reported localities of ancient places. With very few exceptions, therefore, I pass over in silence the monkish traditions.

On the east side of the valley of Jehoshaphat

* Robinson's Bib. Res. ii. 16.

are four remarkable tombs, hewn out of the
solid rock, to which are now given the names
of Jehoshaphat, Absalom, St. James, and
Zecharias. In the earlier notices of these,
different names are assigned to them ; so that
all that is said about them is mere conjecture.
A thought struck me in regard to them, which
I merely throw out as a possibility, without
pretending to assert its correctness. These
tombs are held in high estimation by the Jews;
they visit them and pray beside them. I met
many Jews at the tomb of Zecharias, some of
whom were inscribing their names upon it.
They, in common with the Christians, call this
the tomb of Zechariah, the son of Barachiah.
I regret that I omited to ask them by what
name they call the one allotted by the Christians to St. James. The style of architecture,
being mingled Grecian and Egyptian, shows
them to be comparatively modern. " If they
existed prior to the destruction of Jerusalem,"
says Robinson, " they are probably to be re-
ferred to the times of the Herods."* Sup-

* Bib. Researches, i. 521.

ing this to be the case, their construction
would, in the time of our Saviour, be a recent
event; and as we know, that even under their
vassalage to the Romans, there were some rich
men among the Jews, such as Joseph of Arimathea, who had tombs for themselves which
they had "hewn out in the rock,"* it is at
least not improbable that all, or some of these
tombs, may have been erected, or, more cor-
rectly speaking, "hewn out," by the more
wealthy of the Scribes and Pharisees, in honour
of some of the prophets. May it not be in
allusion to these very tombs that our Lord
says, "Woe unto you Scribes and Pharisees,
hypocrites! because ye build the tombs of the
prophets, and garnish the sepulchres of the
righteous, and say, If we had been in the days
of our fathers, we would not have been partakers with them in the blood of the prophets."
Then, after relating how they would deal with
the first preachers of the gospel, He adds:
"That upon you may come all the righteous
blood shed upon the earth, from the blood of

* Matt. xxvii. 60.

righteous Abel, unto the blood of Zacharias, son of Barachias :"* one of the prophets to whose memory they had lately made a monument.

It is painful to the child of God to behold the mosque of the false prophet stand where that temple once stood, in which God manifested his presence by the shechinah ; it is melancholy to see God's ancient people in darkness and ignorance, oppressed and despised, in their own city ; but it is even more sad to see there the mixture of folly, falsehood, and wickeducss, that calls itself Christianity. I have elsewhere mentioned† the effect necessarily produced on the minds of my brethren, the Jews, by the false representation of the Christian religion exhibited to them by the Papists in Poland and Germany ; but here, where the Lord from heaven Himself introduced a new and spiritual dispensation, the exhibition of folly and blasphemy presented by the Greek and Romish churches, exceeds, perhaps, what is to be met with elsewhere. The palm of

* Matt. xxiii. 29, 35.
† Brief Sketch of the Present State and Future Expectation of the Jews.

superiority in evil, however, must be accorded to the Greek and other Eastern churches, whose exhibitions during Easter have no parallel except in the rites of the heathen. As I did not arrive in Jerusalem until three weeks after the Greek Easter, I did not myself witness the extraordinary scenes that are yearly enacted in the church of the Holy Sepulchre: but my friend, Mr. Calman, who has resided several years in Jerusalem, has kindly permitted me to publish a letter written by him to a friend in England, immediately after he had witnessed the melancholy and revolting spectacle.

During the Greek Easter week, Jerusalem is resorted to by thousands of pilgrims, not only from all parts of Palestine and Syria, but even from such distant places as Syra, Smyrna, and Constantinople. Last Easter it was computed that not less than ten thousand persons were present. This holy fair is celebrated with revellings and jollity, nearly akin to those of secular meetings that go under the same name.

The church of the Holy Sepulchre is a pile of clumsy buildings, professing to cover, in most convenient juxta-position, both Calvary

and the tomb of Christ ; and furnished after
the most approved fashion of monkish falsehood and audacity, with every thing that can be
thought of, connected with the great event
thus shamefully desecrated ; of all of which, it
may be said truly, in the words of the Scotch
deputation, " the wonder is, that the writers
('of travels') should have been so careful in
describing what no serious mind can regard
but as ' lying wonders.' "*

This church, and the relics it contains, are
the great objects of attraction to the pilgrims ;
and here, on the last day of the week, is performed the impious juggle of the holy fire.
Omitting the first part of Mr. Calman's letter,
I extract the portion that relates to this blasphemous imposture of, what the advocates of
apostolic succession denominate, " a sister
church."

" Having thus given a brief outline of the
edifice, I shall now proceed to describe the
ceremony I have alluded to, namely, that of
the miraculous Greek fire, which takes place

* Narrative of a Mission of Enquiry to the Jews,
p. 185.

on the Saturday of the Greek Easter week ;
and which serves, in the hands of the Greek
and Armenian priests, the same purpose that
the keys of Peter do in the hands of his skil-
ful successors, the Popes : it unlocks every
coffer and purse of the pilgrims, and renders
them at the disposal of the inventors and per-
petrators of this lying wonder.

" To notice all that was passing within the
church of the Holy Sepulchre during the space
of more than twenty-four hours, would be next
to impossible ; because it was one continuation
of shameless madness and rioting, which would
have been a disgrace to Greenwich and Smith-
field fairs. Only suppose for a moment the
mighty edifice crowded to excess with fanatic
pilgrims of all the Eastern churches, who, instead of lifting up pure hands to God, without
wrath and quarrelling, are led by the petty
jealousies about the precedency which they
should maintain in the order of their proces-
sions, into tumults and fightings, which can
only be quelled by the scourge and whip of
the followers of the false prophet. Suppose
further, these thousands of devotees running

from one extreme to the other,—from the
extreme of savage irritation to that of savage
enjoyment, of mutual revellings and feastings;
like Israel of old, who, when they made the
golden calf, were eating, and drinking, and
rising up to play. Suppose troops of men,
stripped half naked to facilitate their actions,
running, trotting, jumping, galloping, to and
fro, the breadth and length of the church;
walking on their hands with their feet aloft in
the air; mounting on one another's shoulders,
some in a riding, and some in a standing position, and by the slightest push are all sent
down to the ground in one confused heap,
which made one fear for their safety. Suppose
further, many of the pilgrims dressed in fur
caps, like the Polish Jews, whom they feigned
to represent, and whom the mob met with all
manner of contempt and insult, hurrying them
through the church as criminals who had been
just condemned, amid loud execrations and
shouts of laughter, which indicated that Israel
is still a derision amongst these heathens, by
whom they are still counted as sheep for the
slaughter. All these, and similar proceedings

marked the introduction of this holy miraculous
fire ; and when questioned about the propriety
of such conduct within a Christian place of
worship, and with the name of religion, the
priests will tell you, that they once tried to get
quit of these absurdities, and the holy fire was
withdrawn in consequence of it !

" About two o'clock on Saturday afternoon,
the preparations for the appearance of the
miraculous fire commenced.   The multitude,
who had been heretofore in a state of frenzy
and madness, became a little more quiet ; but
it proved a quiet that precedes a thunderstorm.
Bishops and priests in their full canonicals,
then issued forth from their respective quarters,
with flags and banners, crucifixes and crosses,
lighted candles and smoking censers, to join or
rather to lead, a procession, which moved
thrice round the church, invoking every picture, altar, and relic, in their way, to aid them
in obtaining the miraculous fire.   The procession then returned to the place from whence
it started, and two grey-headed bishops, the
one of the Greek, the other of the Armenian
church, were hurled by the soldiers through

the crowd, into the apartment which communi-
cates with that of the Holy Sepulchre, where
they locked themselves in; there the marvellous fire was to make its first appearance,
and from thence issue through the small circular windows and the door, for the use of the
pilgrims. The eyes of all, men, women, and
children, were now directed towards the Holy
Sepulchre with an anxious suspense, awaiting
the issue of their expectation.

" The mixed multitude, each in his or her own
language, were pouring forth their clamorous
prayers to the Virgin and the saints, to inter-
cede for them on behalf of the object for which
they were assembled; and the same were ten-
fold increased by the fanatic gestures and the
waving of the garments by the priests of the
respective communions who were interested in
the holy fire, and who were watching by the
above-mentioned door and circular windows,
with torches in their hands, ready to receive
the virgin flame of the heavenly fire, and convey it to their flocks. In about twenty minutes from the time the bishops locked themselves in the apartment of the Holy Sepulchre

the miraculous fire made its appearance through
the door and the two small windows, as expected.   The priests were the first who lighted
their torches, and they set out on a gallop in
the direction of their lay brethren : but some
of these errandless and profitless messengers
had the misfortune to be knocked down by
the crowd, and had their firebrands wrested
out of their hands ; but some were more for-
tunate, and safely reached their destination,
around whom the people flocked like bees, to
have their candles lighted.   Others, however,
were not satisfied at having the holy fire
second hand, but rushed furiously towards the
Holy Sepulchre, regardless of their own safety,
and that of those who obstructed their way ;
though it has frequently happened that persons
have been trampled to death on such occasions.
Those who were in. the galleries let down their
candles by cords, and drew them up when
they had succeeded in their purpose.   In a
few minutes thousands of flames were ascending, the smoke and the heat of which rendered
the church like the bottomless pit.   To satisfy
themselves, as well as to convince the Latins,

(who grudge so profitable as well as so effectual a piece of machinery being in the hands of the schismatical Greeks and Armenians, and one which augments the power of the priest and the revenue of the convents, and who, therefore, exclaim against the miraculous fire,) the pilgrims, women, as well as men, shamefully expose their bare bosoms to the action of the flame of their lighted candles, to make their adversaries believe the miraculous fire differs from an ordinary one, in being perfectly harmless. The two bishops, who a little while before locked themselves in the apartment of the Holy Sepulchre, now sallied forth out of it. When the whole multitude had their candles lighted, the bishops were caught by the crowd, lifted upon their shoulders, and carried to their chapels amidst loud and triumphant acclamations. They soon, however, re-appeared, at the head of a similar procession as the one before, as a pretended thank-offering to the Almighty for the miraculous fire vouchsafed, thus daring to make God a partaker in their lie. An express messenger was immediately

R

sent off to Bethlehem, the birth-place of Christ, to inform the brethren there, and to invite them also to offer up their tribute of thanks for the transcendant glory of the day. Thus closed the lying wonders of the holy week of Easter."

Such is the picture of Christianity annually presented to the eyes of the Mohammedans; and though no Jews are permitted to witness it, they hear of it from their Musselman neighbours, with whom they are on more friendly terms than they are with the Christians. Surely the very first act of any mission to the Jews ought to have been to testify against, and to repudiate all alliance with those apostate Eastern churches, in order to convince them that they came to teach a Christianity very different from any thing that goes by that name in Jerusalem; and therefore every Christian must regret this not being the case with the present mission there, but that the following letter was sent instead:

" Letter commendatory from the Most Rev. the Lord Archbishop of Canterbury, &c.

" To the Right Reverend our Brothers in Christ, the Prelates and Bishops of the ancient and Apostolic Churches in Syria, and the countries adjacent, greeting in the Lord.

" We, William, by Divine Providence, Archbishop of Canterbury, Primate of all England, and Metropolitan, most earnestly commend to your brotherly love the Right Rev. Michael Solomon Alexander, Doctor in Divinity, whom we, being well assured of his learning and piety, have consecrated to the office of a bishop of the united Church of England and Ireland, according to the ordinances of our holy and Apostolic Church, and having obtained the consent of our Sovereign Lady the Queen, have sent out to Jerusalem, with authority to exercise spiritual jurisdiction over the clergy and congregations of our church, which are now, or which hereafter may be, established in the countries above mentioned. And in order to prevent any misunderstanding in regard to this our purpose, we think it right to make known to you, that we have charged the said bishop our brother not to intermeddle in any way with the jurisdiction of the prelates or other ecclesiastical dignitaries bearing rule in the churches of the East, but to show them due reverence and honour ; and to be ready on all occasions, and by all the means in his power, to promote a mutual interchange of respect, courtesy, and kindness. We have good reason to believe that our brother is willing, and will feel himself in conscience bound, to follow these our instructions ; and we beseech you, in the name of our Lord Jesus Christ, to receive him as a brother, and to assist him, as opportunity may offer, with your good offices.

"We trust that your Holiness will accept this communication as a testimony of our respect and affection, and of our hearty desire to renew that amicable intercourse with the ancient churches of the East, which has been suspended for ages, and which, if restored, may have the effect, with the blessing of God, of putting an end to divisions which have brought the most grievous calamities on the church of Christ.

"In this hope, and with sentiments of the

highest respect for your Holinesses, we have affixed our archiepiscopal seal to this letter, written with our hand at our palace of Lambeth, on the twenty-third day of November, in the year of our Lord one thousand eight hundred and forty-one."

All this to these reverend impostors, — to these "Holinesses," who set fire to a few ounces of alcohol, and then solemnly thank God for having sent a miraculous flame down from heaven!

I cannot suppose that the Archbishop of Canterbury, or any of those concerned, were fully aware of the state of those churches whose ministers were thus addressed; but how grievous is it that the head of the mission at Jerusalem should have been introduced under such auspices; that such a document should have been published and promulgated in Arabic, that Jews and Mohammedans might see the "amicable intercourse!" I am well aware of the obloquy to which I expose myself by these remarks; but I seek not to please men; "for if I yet pleased men, I should not be the servant of Christ." If I sought a life

of ease, I should glide along with the current
of public opinion, and "prophesy smooth
things;" but I dare not speak of any thing
otherwise than as God sees I think of it. Nor
am I intermeddling with that which is no
concern of mine; I have to bear the shame of
this unholy alliance among my unconverted
brethren, who are but ill-informed in regard
to the sectional distinctions of the Christian
church, and therefore naturally hold one
Christian answerable for the views and opinions of another. It is true I could tell my
brethren in Jerusalem, that the church to
which the mission belongs is very different
indeed from the Eastern churches; but what
avails such an assertion in the face of a public
document that gives not the slightest hint of
any such difference? It may be said that the
lives of the missionaries will show their Christianity to be different. Most willingly do I
admit this; but to be able to judge of their
walk and conversation, would augur a degree
of intercourse from which the more pious
Jews will shrink. Any difference they do
perceive, they do not lay to the account of

their Christianity, but to their belonging to England.

Let it not be said that in these remarks I am actuated by enmity to the London Jews' Society. Whatever faults and mistakes it may have committed it has been the instrument of much good to the Jews, and by its distribution of Hebrew New Testaments, has in many quarters stirred up a spirit of inquiry, of which we shall hereafter see the fruits. As little am I actuated by any enmity to the Church of England. Why, of all sections of the Christian church, should I feel enmity at the only one that for many years did any thing for the welfare of Israel? I speak as a member of the church of Christ, to my fellow members of the church of Christ; urging them to prayer and consideration, as to how this stumbling-block is to be removed out of the way of my brethren, the Jews. Let them remember how God judged Israel of old, when they had any alliance with the idolatry of the nations; and having established themselves on that Zion which the Lord loveth, and hath chosen, to put His name there, let them tremble at appearing partakers of other men's sins, lest God should blow upon all their efforts, and visit them with His sore displeasure.

I am forced, very much against my inclination, thus to state my views in regard to the mission in Jerusalem. Many Christians, who are its friends and well-wishers, have urged me to do so; and had I passed it over in silence, my motives for so doing would have been misconstrued. The great and important lesson the Jews ought to be taught, is, that Christianity is a spiritual religion; an internal power, regulating the heart and conduct; and that all outward ordinances and arrangements, though useful as instruments, are in themselves of no value, apart from this internal principle. The apostate Eastern churches, therefore, consisting only of outward forms (to say nothing of their false doctrine), ought at once to have been disowned; and while their Bishops might have been treated with courtesy as men, should never have been recognized as ministers of Christ. The very simplest mode of worship, also, of which the Church of England admits, ought, according to this view, to have been adopted, to make the line of demarcation between it and the Eastern churches as broad as possible. A bishop in his full canonicals, preceded by a Janissary with two silver-headed staves, and followed by three robed priests, do not form the best arrangement for convincing the Jews of the simplicity of Christian worship. In this I am not at all speaking as a Nonconformist. A large body of attached members of the Church of England will join me in saying, that there is a wide difference between its services, when conducted in the simplest manner that is consistent with order, and when encumbered with as many outward trappings as its Protestant character will admit of.

It is with the utmost reluctance I make these remarks. Far more agreeable is it to me to testify, that I believe my dear brother, Bishop Alexander, to be a truly Christian man : and who knows what work may yet be allotted to him in the providence of God?

The first Sunday I spent in Jerusalem I saw four of my brethren baptized ; two of them residents there, and two who had been sent thither to be baptized from another of the society's stations. The bishop gave them a touching and excellent address. Most heartily do I say, " The Lord add unto them an hundred fold, and may his eyes see it." And above all, may those he baptizes be members of the true church, and not merely swell the already over-crowded ranks of nominal Christianity!

It is certainly a remarkable sign of the times, that a Jew should be sent out as bishop to Jerusalem by the most powerful nation of the earth. Whatever its spiritual results may be, it is quite evident it is already regarded as a political movement, not only by the Turks, but by the other European powers. Britain had a consul in Jerusalem for three years before any other nation, except Prussia, thought of having the same; but no sooner did she send a bishop than France, Russia, and Austria sent consuls forthwith; and thus in Jerusalem — which is, in a commercial point of view, but a paltry, inland, eastern town, without trade or importance of any kind,—sit the five consuls of the great European powers, looking at one another, it is difficult to say why or wherefore. To use the words of Dr. Keith, in his interesting work recently published : " A country which for previous centuries *no man inquired after*, excites anew the liveliest interest among the greatest of earthly potentates." *

There is a curious fact I learnt in Jerusalem, which was told me with much triumph by some of my brethren. Within the last few years there have been fourteen converts from Christianity to Judaism. What has been the motive of this strange movement I cannot tell ; but it will easily be believed the Jews are delighted to have such a set-off to any conversions effected among them.

But I must linger no longer in Jerusalem. One interesting fact I will mention, and then take my leave of it. There are still lepers dwelling in Jerusalem. Near the Zion gate are some miserable hovels, where the leprous families reside, apart from others, associating and intermarrying only with each other. How forcibly does this recal the remembrance of

* The Land of Israel, p. 476.

Him who spake the word, and the leper was cleansed! Though Jerusalem is favoured more than most Eastern cities, in having two excellent medical men, Dr. Macgowan, of the mission, and Dr. Frankel, a Jewish physician, sent there by Sir Moses Montefiore; yet to the poor leper nothing avails but that "gift of healing" which subsists in the church no longer.

No traveller can visit Jerusalem without being sensible what an acquisition to it the worthy British consul is; whose kind attentions and friendly aid are always at the service even of those who have no claim on them beyond that of being strangers in a strange land. And it would be well if all British residents abroad showed the same example of high-toned morality that Mr. Young exhibits.

On Monday, May 21st, M. and I, in company with Dr. Wilson, of Bombay, and Mr. Graham, Scottish Missionary to the Jews, set off for Bethlehem. On our way we saw the aqueduct that conveyed the water from Solomon's pools to Jerusalem. The next object of interest was Rachel's tomb. The present

building is an ordinary Mohammedan tomb;
but there is every reason to believe that it
occupies the place where "the pillar of Rachel's grave" once stood. The Jews hold it
in high veneration; and make pilgrimages to
pray there. The Mohammedans, who also
venerate it, do not permit the Jews to enter
within it; even Sir Moses Montefiore when
he visited it, was obliged to remain outside.
There is a hole in the wall at which they pray,
so that their voices enter into the tomb. On
considering the situation of this tomb, being
in the highway between Bethlehem and Jerusalem, we can at once understand both the
poetic allusion of the prophet Jeremiah, to
" Rachel weeping for her children," and the
application of it by Matthew to the massacre
of the infants at Bethlehem. Even to this
day may Rachel weep over her children,
" scattered and peeled," " meted out and
trodden down;" but her mourning is not
always to continue: " There is hope in thine
end, saith the Lord, that thy children shall
come again to their own border." *

* Jeremiah xxxi. 17.

S

Bethlehem is about six miles from Jerusalem, and is situated on the slope of a ridge. The valleys and fields around it are tolerably well cultivated, and produce good crops, so it may still be called "a house of bread." How many interesting associations are connected with this spot! Here Naomi and Ruth dwelt on coming from Moab; some of these fields were once the possession of the wealthy Boaz. A portion of his inheritance descended to his grandson Jesse; here David was born; and here, when the fulness of time was come, the Son and Lord of David, the true "Ruler of Israel" was born; — the Lord of glory came into the world He had made, a helpless infant! Mysterious truth! Can we wonder that many should disbelieve it? The real wonder is, that many who profess to believe it, are so indifferent about it. The more we contemplate this wonderful event, the more do we feel that "no man can say that Jesus is the Lord but by the Holy Ghost."*

What a momentous night was that, when

* 1 Cor. xii. 3.

Christ, "the true bread," came down from heaven! I looked with the deepest interest on the fields round Bethlehem, and at a little distance from it, in some of which the shepherds were feeding their flocks when the angel announced the "glad tidings," that a Saviour was born. The inhabitants of Bethlehem are at present all nominally Christian; yet what do they know of Christ? They know no more of Him as a Saviour from sin, as a restorer of the lost image of God in the soul of man, than the Mohammedans around them.

In the church of the convent at Bethlehem is shown the cave of the nativity, as it is called. It is certainly possible that this cave may have been a place for cattle, belonging to an ancient Khan or inn; but it is equally probable that it was fixed upon, in the days of Helena, as the most convenient spot to which they could attach the tradition, without any sufficient warrant for doing so. As the sepulchre of Moses was hidden from the Israelites, so it may be better for us that an air of uncertainty hangs over the precise spots connected both with the birth and the death of Christ; that we may be kept from the worship of the visible, and from attaching peculiar sanctity to any thing material, which has a necessary tendency to weaken our faith in the universal spiritual presence of Christ with His members.

In the birth of Jesus at Bethlehem, we see one of those unintentional coincidences that so strikingly mark the fulfilment of prophecy. Micah had said, by the Spirit, more than seven centuries before: "But thou, Bethlehem-Ephratah, though thou be little among the thousands of Judah, yet out of thee shall he come forth unto me who is to be ruler in Israel; whose goings forth have been from of old, from everlasting." * Whether Mary and Joseph were acquainted with this prophecy, or whether the knowledge of it was confined to the "chief priests and scribes," we cannot tell; however this might be, Mary remained quietly in Nazareth, not taking the fulfilment into her own hands, by a timely removal to Bethlehem. A heathen emperor must issue a decree just at the set time, and thus bring the

* Micah, v. 2.

mother of Jesus to the place appointed for
His birth. Do we not recognize in this the
hand of Him who " seeth the end from the
beginning ? "

St. Jerome lived in the convent at Bethlehem when he translated the Scriptures into
Latin; a cave is shown as the apartment he
occupied when so engaged. Of the absurdities shown by the monks, I shall say nothing
further, than that as every body must be
accommodated with some memorial, Joseph
must needs have an apartment as well as
others; but all they have been able to spare
for him is a mere niche, or hole in the wall,
into which he must have had some difficulty in
squeezing himself.

From Bethlehem we proceeded to the convent of Mar Saba, where M. and I were to
remain for the night, as we intended to pro-
cecd next morning to the Dead Sea. After
about an hour's ride, the country became very
wild and desolate, being the commencement of
the Wilderness of Judea, a large tract of desert
country that stretches along all the west side

of the Dead Sea.   The convent of Mar Saba
is an extraordinary place.   It was founded by
the person whose name it bears at the end of
the fifth century, and has ever since been inhabited by a succession of monks of the Greek
church.   The brook Kedron, which rises, or
I ought to say, which did rise, to the north of
Jerusalem, here has flowed through a deep
ravine, the sides of which are precipitous, and
the convent is built up one side of the ravine ;
the foundation being nearly on the level of the
torrent bed, while the entrance is from the
high ground above.   The bed of the brook
Kedron, like that of nearly all the ancient
rivers of Palestine, is quite dry, merely serving
the purpose of draining off the heavy rains of
winter.   Dr. Wilson called our attention to
this dry channel, stretching uninterruptedly to
the Dead Sea, as being ready prepared for the
"living water" mentioned in Ezek. xlvii.   The
same stream is also alluded to in Zech. xiv. 8 ;
the "former sea" in that verse remaining the
eastern or Dead Sea.   We could fully understand the allusion in that verse : "In summer

and in winter shall it be :" a constantly flowing stream, not as now, the mere rush of a winter's torrent.

We parted with regret from Dr. Wilson and Mr. Graham, who returned to Jerusalem. We were joined by our former fellow-travellers, who were to accompany us to the Dead Sea, and our formidable looking guard, consisting of a Sheik or chief, and fifteen Arabs. It is impossible to take such a journey without a guard; and as to the number of which it is to consist, you are almost entirely at the mercy of the Sheik, with whom you must make the best bargain you can.

Dr. Wilson had perceived among the rocks a small animal, which he thought was the coney of Scripture. M. promised to endeavour to get one for him, which, by the help of the Bedouins, he succeeded in doing. We climbed up to see its nest, which was a hole in the rock, comfortably lined with moss and feathers, answering to the description given of the coney in Psa. civ. 18, and Prov. xxx. 26.

. At five o'clock next morning we left Mar Saba for the Dead Sea. The farther we penetrated into this wilderness, the more sterile and desolate it became; it can only be described by the Scripture phrases, "a terrible wilderness," a "waste and howling wilderness." The narrow track we pursued sometimes followed the undulations of the rocky heights, and sometimes we were hid in mountain passes between them. It was in this "dry and thirsty land, where no water is," that David gave utterance to the sixty-third Psalm. This same desert tract of country seems to have taken different names, according to the towns on which it bordered; as the wilderness of Ziph, the wilderness of Tekoa; and it was through various parts of it that David wandered when he fled from Saul. A large natural cavern, considerably to the south of where we now were, is shown as the cave of Adullam.

But the subject that was uppermost in my mind during the ride in this awful wilderness, was, the character and preaching of John the Baptist. "In these days came John the Baptist preaching in the wilderness of Judea: and the same John had his raiment of camel's

hair, and a leathern girdle about his loins;
and his meat was locusts and wild honey."*
Why does the Holy Spirit tell us the dress
and the food of John? Because John was,
like his father Zacharias, a priest " of the
course of Abia" or Abijah; he had a right
to wear the priestly robe, to be girded with
the ephod, and to feed on the meat of the
sacrifices. Why did he not reside in Jerusalem? Why did he not " execute the priest's
office in the order of his course,—to burn
incense when he went into the temple of the
Lord?" Because he was appointed to be the
forerunner of a new dispensation, in which the
ceremonial priesthood of the few, was to give
place to the spiritual priesthood of the whole
body of believers. He therefore refused his
priestly garments, and put on the ordinary
dress of the wandering Ishmaelite of the
desert; that he might testify to the Priests
and Levites, that " the voice of one that
crieth" must now be listened to because it is
truth, and not because it is announced by a

---

* Matt. iii. 1, 4.

man wearing a certain garment. He lived in the wilderness, thereby to declare that every place was his Bethel; and to show to those who laid so much stress on the locality of the Temple, that the dispensation was at hand, under which, as had been predicted by the prophets, "in every place incense shall be offered" unto the name of the Lord. And while "they which minister about holy things, live of the things of the temple, and they which wait at the altar, are partakers with the altar," John lived on the common food of the desert; his altar was everywhere; and perhaps on some of the very rocks on which my eye rested, he offered up "spiritual sacrifices acceptable to God."

What a strange eccentric being must John have appeared to the priests and the Pharisees of his day! His non-conformity must indeed have scandalized them. Had he been disposed to listen to them, we can imagine how much sage advice they would have given him, about remaining in his calling; how many pleas of additional usefulness, and more extensive influence, they might have urged, to induce him to abandon his divisive courses! But John knew that priesthood had decayed, and "waxed old," and was "ready to vanish away;" and that a dispensation was about to commence, that was not a counterpart, but a contrast to the former; a contrast in so far, that all that was ceremonial and material in the one, was to be succeeded by that which is spiritual and real in the other.

About half-past ten o'clock we reached the Dead Sea. No one can look on this remarkable spot without feeling that the curse rests upon it. It is a salt lake or inland sea, about fifty miles in length, and generally from ten to twelve miles broad. The Arabs call it "the Sea of Lot." "The phenomena around the Dead Sea are such as might naturally be expected from the character of its waters and the region round about,—a naked, solitary, desert. It lies in its deep cauldron, surrounded by lofty cliffs of naked limestone rock, and exposed for seven or eight months in each year to the unclouded beams of a burning sun. Nothing, therefore, but sterility and death-like solitude

can be looked for upon its shores."* The
water is intensely salt, with a bitter, disagreeable, taste. Thick incrustations of salt are
deposited on some parts of its banks, which
the Arabs gather for the use of their families
and flocks. The river Jordan empties itself
into the northern end of it.

The "cities of the plain," are supposed to
have stood at the southern end of this lake;
where there is a hilly ridge that is called by
the Arabs at this day "the stone of Sodom,"
and which they say is "composed wholly of
rock salt, too bitter to be fit for cooking, and
only used sometimes as a medicine for sheep."†
It is impossible to look without awe on this
monument of the "severity of God," especially
in recollecting that the inspired apostles, Peter
and Jude, both refer to it, with a voice of
warning, when speaking of "false teachers,
who privily shall bring in damnable heresies
into the church of Christ.

We bathed in the Dead Sea, and found its

* Robinson's Bib. Researches, ii. 219.
† Ibid. 206.

water extremely buoyant, though perhaps not quite in the degree we had expected. In the autumn, after the long drought of summer, it is probably much more so; and at the north end, where we bathed, it may be in some measure affected by the influx of the fresh water of the Jordan. Dr. Robinson, the most cautious and correct of travellers, who bathed considerably farther south, says : " The water is exceedingly buoyant. Two of us bathed in the sea, and although I could never swim before, either in fresh or salt water, yet here I could sit, stand, lie, or swim in the water without difficulty." *

We next proceeded over a sandy plain, and through scenes of utter desolation, to the banks of the Jordan. The place we visited is said to have been the scene of our Saviour's baptism ; and not far from the same spot the passage of the Israelites must have taken place. Here there are a few shrubs and small trees ; and after so much desolation, any green thing is welcome to the eye ; but I could not help call-

* Robinson's Bib. Researches, ii. 213.

ing to mind the poetical allusions to the "green banks of Jordan," with which hymns abound; and thought the mere shreds and patches of vegetation that are now to be seen on them present a very different picture to the eye.

It is at this place that the Greek pilgrims conclude the festivities of their unhallowed week; men and women, in a state of nudity, promiscuously bathing in the stream. The current is here so rapid, that it is dangerous to do more than dip in at the very edge of the water; those who venture farther are frequently carried down the stream and drowned.

We next proceeded towards Jericho. On our way we must have passed near "Gilgal, in the east border of Jericho," where Joshua and the Israelites encamped after they had crossed Jordan. Here "the reproach of Egypt was rolled away" from them; and here they kept the first passover in the promised land. Their last act before leaving Egypt to set out on their pilgrimage was to celebrate this type of redeeming love; and their first act in Canaan was this memorial of it. They crossed the Jordan on the tenth day of the first month, the day the lamb was to be set apart ; and kept the passover at Gilgal on the fourteenth day of the same month.

No trace of Gilgal, nor of the ancient Jericho, remains. Although the precise site of Jericho cannot be fixed upon, there is no doubt that it was in the immediate vicinity of the place that still bears its name. There is a square tower, called the castle of Jericho, which Robinson supposes to be as recent as the twelfth century ; and there have been notices of the place from Scripture times until now. A filthy Arab village is now the only representative of the once famous Jericho. There is some cultivation in the plain of Jericho, by means of irrigation.

We pitched our tent for the night under the shade of some trees, close by the stream which flows from the Fountain of Elisha. This was an interesting spot, as there is no reason to doubt that the fountain is the very same on which Elisha performed the miracle of healing its waters.*   Even the cautious Robinson

* 2 Kings ii. 19—22.

says : " It is the only one near Jericho, and there is every reason to regard it as the scene of Elisha's miracle."* The water was once " naught," and the ground in consequence of this " barren." Elisha cast a cruse of salt in it, " and said, Thus saith the Lord, I have healed these waters; there shall not be from thence any more dearth or barren land." The word of the Lord standeth sure ; the water is now sweet and pleasant ; and it is the water of this fountain that irrigates the neighbouring crops. When beholding the standing evidence of this miracle, I could not help thinking of the nauseous waters of the Dead Sea ; and asking why we should not take the prophecy literally, that relates to its healing. When Ezekiel saw the vision of the waters that flowed from the sanctuary, his heavenly guide said to him : " These waters issue out toward the east country, and go down into the desert (' the desert or plain of Judah'), and go into the sea ; which being brought forth into the sea, the waters shall be healed."† Then may the

* Robinson's Bib. Res. ii. 283.   † Ezek. xlvii. 8.

" desert rejoice, and blossom as the rose" ; for " every thing shall live whither the river cometh."*

The road from Jericho to Jerusalem is one of the wildest and most dangerous in Palestine, and is still the favourite haunt of robbers ; so that a man cannot even now go " from Jerusalem to Jericho" without the risk of falling " among thieves" ; while the " good Samaritans," alas! are there no longer. It is chiefly on account of this part of the journey that so large an escort is necessary. Shortly before we came, a gentleman travelling this road happened to linger behind the rest of his party, when he was immediately surrounded by robbers, who literally " stripped him of his raiment, and wounded him, and departed."

On Tuesday, the 30th of May, we bade adieu to Jerusalem, and set out for Jaffa, the ancient Joppa. About an hour after we left Jerusalem we were much struck with the beautiful verdure of the trees in the orchards near which we passed; a sight so rare in " this land of

* Ezek. xlvii. 9.

2 T

drought" and barrenness, Such spots vividly call to mind what Palestine was, and what it will yet be. There is no object of interest on this road; Ramleh, the only town we passed through, is traditionally said to be the ancient Arimathea; but there are strong reasons for believing this cannot be the case.

Jaffa is a small seaport town, entirely devoid of interest in itself, but fraught with interesting recollections to the Christian. Here dwelt the benevolent Dorcas, whom Peter raised to life, and restored to her weeping friends. But the most interesting event connected with it is, that here was first revealed " the mystery,—which in other ages was not made known unto the sons of men,—that the Gentiles should be fellow-heirs, and of the same body, and partakers of his promise in Christ by the Gospel."* Hitherto there had been no entrance into the church of God but by the gate of Judaism; but here God showed unto Peter that the middle wall of partition was broken down, and that Jew and Gentile alike

* Eph. iii. 5, 6.

entered into life through faith in Christ.
Peter's monitory dream prepared him to go
with the messengers of Cornelius, nothing
doubting. Cæsarea, which we passed on the
following day, is a small town on the coast,
about thirty miles from Jaffa. Here lived
the devout Cornelius, who was probably a pro-
selyte of the gate; one who believed the revelation of God contained in the Jewish Scriptures, but who had not joined himself to the
Jewish church. This man, from his acquaintance with the Jews, (he " was of good report
among all the nation of the Jews,") must have
heard something of the reputed Messiah, and
of the wonderful things that had happened
among the Jews during the ten preceding
years; and it is possible his mind may have
been exercised on these matters; and the
prayers that came up " for a memorial before
God," may have been prayers for light and
guidance on the subject. His knowledge of
what had transpired was probably very dark
and confused; as those times did not possess
the facilities for knowledge to run to and fro,

that modern ages afford. God answered his prayers, not by immediate illumination of his own mind, but by sending a fellow man to preach the glad tidings to him. And what did Peter tell him? That there was an apostolic church, in connexion with which there was safety, and out of which there was no hope of any thing but certain "uncovenanted mercies"? That in the mysterious rite of water baptism, he should be regenerated, and made a member of this church? He said not one word of all this. He simply narrated the life and death of our blessed Lord and Saviour, and then added; "Through His name, whosoever believeth in Him shall receive remission of sins."* And, as if to show that the outward rite is but the sign, not the instrument of the Spirit's gift, "while Peter yet spake these words, the Holy Ghost fell on all them which heard the word."†

Here was the true Epiphany—the manifestation to the Gentiles. Here was the "middle wall of partition broken 'down," the abolition

* Acts x. 43.　　　† Ibid. ver. 44.

of "the law of commandments contained in ordinances," that Jew and Gentile might be "builded together for an habitation of God through the Spirit."* And Peter, who had heretofore thought it an unlawful thing for a man that is a Jew to keep company, or come unto one of another nation," tarried some time with Cornelius and his Gentile friends.

My dear brethren of the Gentiles, a Peter, a Paul, and a Timothy, a Silas, a Barnabas, and a Phillip, were willing to spend and be spent to preach the Gospel to the Gentiles; they hesitated not to expose themselves to persecution and privation,—to "perils by the heathen, to perils in the city, to perils in the wilderness, to perils in the sea;" they were "in weariness and painfulness, in watchings often, in hunger and thirst, in fastings often, in cold and nakedness."† Israel is now in unbelief, and ye desire that "through your mercy" some of them, at least, "may obtain mercy." O then remember, that for this end something more is needed than an annual guinea subscription.

* Eph. ii. 14, 15, 22.   † 2 Cor. xi. 26, 27.

Our design was to sail from Jaffa to Beyrout. For this purpose nothing was to be had but an open boat manned by Arab sailors. To add to our discomfort, the Italian servant who had hitherto accompanied us, refused to embark with us, being afraid of sea-sickness. He however, brought to us the master of a boat, who professed to speak Italian, and with him a legal agreement was drawn up in due form, which the British vice-consul told us was quite necessary. There was nothing in Jaffa to make us wish to remain there longer than necessary. While at dinner I perceived with dismay the light dress I wore speedily becoming black with vermin ; on complaining of this to our host, he coolly told me that I must have brought them from the house of Simon the tanner, four empty walls we had visited in the morning.

In the evening we embarked in our boat, which was as filthy and uncomfortable as can well be imagined. The master's whole stock of Italian consisted of two words, *Signore* and *buono ;** our communication with him was con-

* *Sir* and *good.*

sequently of a very limited nature. The bottom of the boat was filled with sand, on which we spread our mats and carpet bags, and rested for the night the best way we could.

Next morning we landed at Khaifa, or Haifa, a village at the base of Mount Carmel. After enjoying the luxury of bathing, we procured donkeys, and ascended to the top of Carmel. This is a ridge of no great height, running obliquely from the Mediterranean, in a southeast direction, for nearly eight miles, its highest point being about 1200 feet above the level of the sea, close to which it rises. What an interesting scene of Scripture history did this mount recal! And what a melancholy reflection to think, that after all that God has revealed to man since the days of Elijah, there should still subsist idolatry too near akin to that of the worshippers of Baal! The cry, "O Mary, hear us,"—"O Anna, hear us," is as vain as the cry of "O Baal, hear us;" and the penances of Rome are dictated by the same spirit that led Baal's prophets to "cut them selves after their manner with knives and lan-

cets till the blood gushed out."* Here was
the scene of the early Jewish reformer's testimony; ten days before I had been in the scene
of the later Jewish reformer's testimony, of
him who came "in the spirit and power of
Elias." And what now meets the traveller's
eye on these spots? Two convents, the one of
the Greek, the other of the Romish church.
Each of these has been recently repaired and
adorned by their respective partisans. The
Emperor of Russia lately gave a large sum of
money for repairing and ornamenting Mar
Saba; and the convent on Mount Carmel has
recently been entirely and substantially rebuilt,
chiefly through money from France, and now
looks more like a fortress than the abode of
peaceable monks. How utterly discouraging
to the Christian would be the successive disappointments that have followed every reformation, were it not for the "sure word of prophecy," in which God "hath promised, saying,
Yet once more I shake not the earth only, but

* 1 Kings xviii. 28.

also heaven : And this word, yet once more, signifieth the removing of those things that are shaken, as of things that are made, that those things which cannot be shaken may remain."* Glorious day, when falsehood, and error, and everything that opposeth itself to the truth, shall become "like the chaff of the summer threshing-floor !"

After leaving Carmel we resumed our voyage. The next morning we passed close to Tyre, the once mighty city, now the abode of a few fishermen, so literally has the word of the Lord been fulfilled : " I will make thee like the top of a rock; thou shalt be a place to spread nets upon."† We also passed Sidon, where Paul was permitted to land when on his voyage to Rome as a prisoner, having " liberty to go unto his friends to refresh himself."‡ Alas! it would be little refreshment to the Christian's spirit to visit Sidon now ! " The town stands upon a high rising ground, which projects a considerable way into the sea. It is enclosed by a high fortified wall on the eastern

* Heb. xii. 26, 27.

† Ezek. xxvi. 14.   ‡ Acts xxvii. 3.

side, and two mosques tower over the other buildings of the town."*

After two tedious nights and days in our open boat, we at length landed at Beyrout, and were kindly received by our excellent friends there. Beyrout is a bustling town, of about fifteen thousand inhabitants, and contrasted with the stillness and desolation of Palestine, gives one at first the idea of a return to civilised life; but this delusion is of short duration; it is but a dirty Turkish town, although two-thirds of the inhabitants are nominally Christians.

Some of my dear friends in England having, as well as myself, taken a deep interest in the cause of education in Syria, I made it my business to obtain all the information I could on the subject, both from the European and native residents there, and by personally visiting the schools. And I feel it an act of common justice, to give the credit of any thing that is done there in the way of education, to those to whom alone it is due, the American mission-

* Narrative of a Mission of Enquiry to the Jews, p. 340.

aries. These excellent men have laboured there
for about twenty years; endeavouring, by the
establishment of schools, and instructing the
adult natives as they have opportunity, to im-
prove the spiritual and moral condition of the
Arabs, the professors of various kinds of spu-
rions Christianity. Their efforts have been
much interrupted by the unsettled political
state of the country; but they have still per-
severed, and we may hope that in due season
they will reap more abundant fruit than they
have yet been enabled to do. Through their
instructions many of the youths in Beyrout are
well acquainted with English; most, if not all,
the Syrian young men, who have come to this
country from Beyrout during the last few years,
owe their education wholly to the American
missionaries. They established the only female
school ever attempted at Beyrout, to which
Mrs. Smith, the wife of one of the missionaries, devoted herself with an assiduity that
injured her health, and led to her premature
removal from earthly labour. This day school
they have been obliged to discontinue, since
the establishment of the camp of Albanian

oldiers; but there are several young women taken under the roof of the different missionaries, who are carefully instructed in whatever is needful to render them useful in this world, as well as in the things that pertain to their eternal welfare.

The missionaries have a printing press, at which they print portions of Scripture, and books and tracts on evangelical Christianity. "The printing in the year 1841 amounted to 636,000 pages, nearly half of which were portions of the sacred Scriptures. The books and tracts distributed exceeded nine thousand, and nearly eight thousand of these have been distributed in Beyrout."* All this activity has at length stirred up the Greek church to jealousy; and they have got rival schools, and a rival printing press. There is a school of 150 boys, under the superintendence of the Greek bishop : and another small school, containing about sixteen younger boys. These schools, of course, are taught by members of the Greek church, and the children attending

* Thirty-third Annual Report of the American Board of Commissioners for Foreign Missions. 1842.

them are taught prayers to the Virgin, and all
the other errors of that apostate community.
In addition to Arabic, they are taught a little
Italian, but no English is taught.   Both these
schools we visited ; and though it is always
pleasing to see any amount of real knowledge
communicated, and the mere art of reading is
an invaluable acquisition, we could not but feel
that every child sent there, who might otherwise have gone to receive the truly evangelical
instruction of the American missionaries, is
thereby deprived of the oportunity of hearing
of that " true light," which alone can illumine
his darkness.   Surely it is folly to talk of the
Greek church holding all the essentials of
truth ; what does it signify, practically, what a
church *holds,* if it does not *teach* the truth ?

The printing press belonging to the Greek
church, is worked by some of the young men
whom the American missionaries instructed in
the art of printing.   These faithful servants of
God have much to suffer from the ingratitude
of those to whose welfare they devote their
best energies.   Many on whom they have be-

stowed almost paternal care and attention, "go back, and walk no more with them."

Their services in Arabic are generally attended by about forty persons, with the serious and devout appearance of many of whom I was much pleased. The missionaries do not begin their instructions by attacking the errors of the Greek church; they set before them simply the pure doctrines of the gospel; and no sooner do the people receive these, than they feel it impossible to remain any longer in connexion with a system of error.

They have a missionary station among the Druzes on Mount Lebanon; and there, as well as in Beyrout, have the useful appendage of a pious physician; or, I should rather say, the useful appendage of medical skill; for the physicians themselves, as well as their wives, are, in every sense of the word, missionaries. We paid an interesting visit to this station, and found Mrs. Van Dyck, the wife of the physician, engaged in the instruction of three young Druze princesses, as they are called, the daughters of some of the Druze chiefs. There

was an appearance of propriety in the de-
meanour of these girls, that showed the good
effects of Mrs. Van Dyck's influence.   I must
again repeat, in opposition to the hasty and
incorrect statements of some travellers who
have not taken the trouble to examine for
themselves, that there is not, nor ever was, any
female school in Beyrout or the neighbour-
hood, except the one already alluded to, as
having been established by the American
missionaries ; that there is nothing whatsoever
doing for female education except by them ;
and that there is no evangelical or protestant
religious instruction communicated to the native population, either male or female, except
by those laborious and excellent persons, of
whom some recent travellers in these parts
take no more notice in their printed narratives
than if they did not exist.

While we were with Mrs. Van Dyck, some
of the elder Druze princesses came in, wearing
the tantour or horn, which has a most extraordinary appearance.   A silver horn, about
two feet in length, is firmly bound round the
head, and a white veil thrown over it ; while

from the back of the head hangs down a bunch
of tassels, ornamented with silver, which
weighs several pounds.

One of the Druze princes or Sheiks invited
us into his house, and said, in a tone of interest and anxiety: "When will England come
and take possession of us? We are in a miserable state of confusion and strife; will not
England take pity upon us?" This rough
warrior, accustomed all his life to the broils
and petty warfare of half-savage life, seems at
length to possess that craving for guidance
which a recent writer represents as the feeling
of the uneducated masses of every country at
present: "He would fain (though as yet he
knows it not) find for himself a superior that
should wisely and lovingly govern. It is for a
manlike place and relation in this world, where
he sees himself a man, that he struggles. At
bottom, may we not say it is even for this:
That guidance and government, which he cannot give himself, which in our so complex
world he can no longer do without, might be
afforded him."* The feeling expressed by

* Chartism. By T. Carlyle, p. 22.

this Druze chief is very general throughout Palestine. It is to be regretted that international etiquette prevents England from complying with a desire so generally felt.

With regard to the project of some benevolent persons in this country, of benefitting Syria by means of a native agency, I will take the liberty of saying, what every European resident in Beyrout will confirm, that in the present state of the country, a mechanical education would be much better suited for this purpose than a literary one. And the expectation of doing any thing whatsoever through the co-operation of the Greek priests, I must believe to be a mere chimera. If any portion of the Greek church is to be improved, it must be by another Luther coming out of her, and testifying against her ; laying down his life if need be, for the testimony of Jesus. And I would really dispel an illusion, caused by the halo which the word *bishop* throws around the personages to whom it is applied. In this country, it is true, a bishop is always a gentleman, and a man of education ; but in Syria a bishop is generally an ignorant Greek, almost as dirty and degraded as the Arab population around him.

Before leaving Beyrout, we paid a visit to the Pasha, which highly amused us. He was seated on his divan, with his feet tucked under him, in the usual Oriental fashion ; he wore a loose robe, like a dressing-gown, and a high red cap on his head. The only article of furniture in his apartment was a large English arm-chair, which some one had presented to him ; but this was evidently more for ornament than use. Several attendants stood at the lower end of the room, with their eyes steadily fixed upon him, so that with the slightest movement of his hand he could signify his wishes to them. It was a complete illustration of the text, " As the eyes of servants look unto the hands of their masters."*

Coffee and pipes having been brought in, the Pasha began to inquire relative to the subject that seemed uppermost in his mind in regard to England,—the aerial machine. He asked all manner of questions about it, and

* Psalm cxxiii. 2.

seemed to labour under a sort of dread that
the English would, ere long, come flying
through the air, and take possession of Syria.
We mentioned to him the Thames Tunnel, as
another of the wonderful works of England;
but this did not appear to impress him so
much; and, by way of a set off to it, he asked
us whether we had ever seen the bridge at
Constantinople; seeming to think a road over
the water quite as wonderful as a road under it.

As my object is not to describe persons, but
things, I have not adopted the prevalent custom of travellers, that of mentioning and eulo-
gising every person they happen to meet with;
but I cannot take leave of Beyrout without acknowledging the kindness of Mr. Wildenbruch,
the Prussian Consul-General, whom I met as a
stranger, and from whom I parted as from an
old friend.

From Beyrout we proceeded in a small sail-
ing vessel to Alexandria, where we only remained a few days. I therefore saw very little
of the country where my fathers were in
bondage; but a very cursory observation en-
ables one to see that its own inhabitants are in

bondage to sin and Satan. It is indeed the land "where death and darkness reign;" but they shall not reign there always, for a day is coming when "the Lord shall be known to Egypt, and the Egyptians shall know the Lord in that day, whom the Lord of Hosts shall bless, saying, Blessed be Egypt, my people."*

We left Alexandria by the steamer on the 20th of June, and on the 11th of July, after five months of pleasant association together, my esteemed fellow-traveller and myself had the happiness of again setting foot in England, his native, and my adopted, country, much gratified with having seen so many interesting places, and thankful for the gracious protection we had enjoyed in all our wanderings.

And now, having been permitted to behold the desolation of my father-land, to witness its moral and physical degradation, what, it may be asked, is the impression left on the mind? A feeling of hope and expectation, that as the night is so dark, the dawn must be near. When Isaiah was told by the Lord, of the

* Isaiah xix. 21, 25.

grossness of heart, the heaviness of ear, and the blindness of eye, that should come upon his people, he inquired how long this was to continue: "Then said I, Lord, how long? And He answered, Until the cities be wasted without inhabitant, and the houses without man, and the land be utterly desolate, and the Lord have removed men far away, and there be a great forsaking in the midst of the land." All this has come to pass. Shall we not, then, confidently expect the speedy fulfilment of the Lord's gracious promises to His people Israel? "Thus saith the Lord God, O mountains of Israel, ye shall shoot forth your branches, and yield your fruit to my people of Israel, for they are at hand to come. For behold, I am for you, and I will turn unto you, and ye shall be tilled and sown; and I will multiply men upon you, all the house of Israel, even all of it; and the cities shall be inhabited, and the wastes shall be builded. And I will multiply upon you man and beast; and they shall encrease and bring fruit; and I will settle you after your old estates, and will do better unto you than at your beginnings; and ye shall know that I am the Lord."*

But the restoration of Israel is connected with the close of the Gentile dispensation. "Jerusalem shall be trodden down of the Gentiles, until the times of the Gentiles be fulfilled."† Whatever may be meant by the accomplishment of the times of the Gentiles, we may venture to say that it does not mean a time of outward ease, and worldly prosperity, such as many of the professing churches of Christ now enjoy; "for there shall be great tribulation, such as was not since the beginning of the world to this time, no, nor ever shall be."‡ In this highly favoured land, I never can look on the luxury of the rich, contrasted with the miserable destitution of the poor, without remembering God's threatening upon "them that dwell carelessly in the isles."§ How well does the description of the state of those that were "at ease in Zion," previous to its day of visitation, apply to many of the higher class of society in England at

* Ezek. xxxvi 7—11. † Luke xxi. 24.
‡ Mat. xxiv. 21. § Ezek. xxxix. 6.

this day! "Ye that put far away the evil day, that lie upon beds of ivory, and stretch themselves upon their couches, and eat the lambs out of the flock, and the calves out of the midst of the stall; that chant to the sound of the viol, and invent to themselves instruments of music like David ; that drink wine in bowls, and anoint themselves with the chief ointments ; but they are not grieved for the affliction of Joseph."* The affliction of their poor brethren is but a passing thought to many of the great and affluent: when the cry of the poor disturbs their repose, they start up; throw -him an alms, and then think of him no more. This is not that wise consideration of the case of the poor to which God has attached a blessing. The condition of the labouring poor is viewed through the medium of party politics, instead of being calmly pondered as in the sight of a heart-searching God. O that the great and noble of the land would regard this as the chief work they have to do at the present crisis ; that they would direct their efforts not merely to alleviate the effects of poverty, but to discover and remove the cause! "Ye have heaped treasure together for the last days. Ye have lived in pleasure on the earth, and been wanton."* Let the complaints of the poor and needy arouse you, before their cries enter "into the ears of the Lord of Sabaoth." "It may be a lengthening of thy tranquility." It may stay impending judgments, like the timely repentance of Nineveh. "And God saw their works, that they turned from their evil way; and God repented of the evil that He had said that He would do unto them, and He did it not."† He whose first coming was in poverty and affliction, will come again in power and glory, when he shall "judge the poor of the people; he shall save the children of the needy, and shall break in pieces the oppres. sor."‡

I by no means wish to encourage in the poor the erroneous notion that the rich are necessarily hard-hearted, and indifferent to their sufferings; or to afford them an excuse for the indulgence of bitter and unkind feelings

* James v. 4.   † Jonah iii. 10.   ‡ Psalm lxxii. 4.

against those who are providentially placed in a station superior to their own. Inequality of outward circumstances has subsisted in the world from the very earliest ages ; and no contrivance of man can ever remove this inequality ; though, doubtless, many of its evils might be remedied. The Christian poor, especially, have little cause to murmur at those " light afflictions which are but for a moment." Think, dear friends, what an eternal weight of glory is before you ! Shall we, who are citizens of the heavenly Jerusalem, fret ourselves on account of the vanity and folly, the heartlessness and oppression, of those who know not God ? Those who do know Him, whether rich or poor, will never oppress or neglect their fellow creatures, and least of all, their brethren in Christ.

Throughout the whole of Scripture, God represents Himself as the friend and protector of the poor. What a source of comfort is this to him whose heart feels its own bitterness,—to him who hath " no help of man at all !" Let the poor of Christ's flock rejoice in the many assurances of their Lord's special care over

them; and let them "rejoice in hope of the
glory of God;" "looking for that blessed hope,
even the glorious appearing of the great God,
and our Saviour, Jesus Christ,"* when "they
shall obtain joy and gladness, and sorrow and
sighing shall flee away."†

* Titus ii. 13.   † Isaiah xxxv. 10.

THE JEWS.

Having already exceeded my limits, I must condense my account of my brethren as much as possible. A lengthened account of conversations held with them would neither be interesting nor useful; as in speaking on the same subject, to the same class of persons, there must always be a great similarity both in the objections urged and the arguments employed. In speaking of the Jews on the Continent of Europe, therefore, I will divide them into three classes, and narrate the conversation held with one of each class, which may serve as a fair specimen of the whole.

1. THE UNLEARNED.

I begun to converse with a poor Jewess by telling her that I was on my way to Jerusalem, the " city of our solemnities," where our fore-

fathers, in the days of their glory, met to
worship the God of Israel. When I proceeded
from this to something of a more personal nature, she said, "O Sir, I do not wish to change
my religion; our religion is the oldest and
best; I would not change it for all the money
in the world." I then tried to convince the
poor woman that she had no religion at all; no
knowledge of the God whom she professed to
worship; no acquaintance either with Moses
or the prophets. She said she can be guided
by those who are learned and pious; that it is
not for such as she to trouble themselves with
matters that are above their capacity. In
short, she showed a degree of dutiful submission to her church that would have delighted a
Tractarian beyond measure. I see not what
he could have done in such circumstances, but
to leave her in quiet possession of her errors.
Perhaps he would urge, that being a Jewess,
ignorant of Christianity, she must be instructed
in it. Doubtless; but in what way could I do
this but by pressing upon her, in the stongest
manner, her personal responsibility to God;
the necessity of examining and endeavouring

to ascertain what God has revealed to man for his salvation. The first step to be taken was to seek to overturn this blindfold submission to a church ; to convince her that her soul was in danger, and that she must answer at the judgment-seat for her refusal to examine what is truth. How congenial to the depraved human heart is this submission to authority in matters of religion,—this shifting the responsibility from ourselves to any spiritual agent who will transact the business for us! The mighty influence of priestcraft in all ages ceases to astonish us when we reflect how willing men are universally to become its dupes. Ignorance is cherished, as affording immunity from the trouble of investigation. "The book is delivered to him that is not learned, saying, Read this, I pray thee; and he saith, I am not learned."*

2. THE TALMUDICAL RABBI.

This class and the last are two extremes that meet in one common point, reverence for tra-

* Isaiah xxix. 12.

dition. In conversing with a French Talmudist,
I was surprised at his using a line of argument
I had never heard resorted to by any other
Rabbi. He seemed well acquainted with Christian writings ; and as some Christians in the
present day appeal to Jewish customs in support of their views, he was disposed to avail
himself in a similar way of the practice of
Christians. In defending Jewish opinions and
observances, founded merely on tradition, he
said that Christians also have many ceremonies
they can only support by tradition. To this I
replied, that the fact of Christians having committed the same error as the Jews, does not
make it less an error, and that the supporters
of tradition, whether Jews or Gentiles, are
committing the sin of adding to the words of
God, and thereby saying that His authoritative
revelation of His will to man is not sufficiently
plain or copious, but must be helped out by
tradition ; which, instead of bearing upon it
the stamp of the wisdom of God, in most cases
plainly shows itself to be only the foolish va-
garies of men. He then pleaded the respect
due to the Talmud, on account of its antiquity,

and its being the exponent of the views of wise and learned men. I told him that in matters of religion I could receive nothing on any plea but that of its being the truth of God, and pointed out to him several instances in which the tradition alters and annuls the original intent of the command of God. The Rabbi then charged me with pride in setting up my own wisdom in opposition to that of the wise ancients, and presuming to judge for myself what is truth. I told him the revelation made by God in the Holy Scriptures is addressed to every individual; that it is meant to be understood by men, and that every man is bound to make himself acquainted with it. All this he admitted. I said he ought not, then, to blame me for having studied the word of God with the prayer of David,—"Open, thou, mine eyes, that I may behold wondrous things out of thy law." I assured him that whosoever does this with an earnest desire to know the mind of God, will be guided by Him into all truth; but that if we only read the Scriptures in order to get support for favourite opinions, and preconceived notions, we are led to believe

a lie, and to cling to it. I then read to him
from the Bible some of the awful warnings
given to the Israelites by Moses, and the prophetic denunciations uttered against them, and
reminded him how very literally these had
been fulfilled, urged upon them the necessity of
taking Scripture in its plain and literal meaning. I also reminded him that from ancient
times the teachers of Israel had been those
who caused them to err, and read to him some
of the solemn denunciations of Isaiah and Jeremiah against the teachers of error. I then
appealed to him as a teacher of Israel on the
awful responsibility he incurred, if, as I fully
believed, the tendency of all his instructions
was to keep them from the true knowledge of
God. On this he began to cry out vehemently
that I should not persuade him to be a Christian; that Christians were more wicked than
Jews; with much more in the same strain;
when I interrupted him by saying that we had
not yet come to this advanced stage of the argument; that I wished first to prove to him
that he was not a true Israelite. The rest of
our conversation I do not feel it needful to

narrate. If we in a measure succeed in removing Talmudical objections to Christianity,
it is still but gaining access into the outer court
of the fortress : the stronghold itself, man's
evil heart of unbelief, has yet to be assailed ;
and its power of resistance to the truth is very
much the same in all men.

3. The Freethinker.

This is a class that I believe is on the increase among the Jews. I heard from a Christian friend, of a Jew, who had an office in the
Synagogue, who he thought was willing to
listen to the Gospel. I invited him to my
hotel. I expressed to him the interest I take
in my brethren, and my anxiety for their welfare. "What do you call their welfare?" he
asked. I spoke to him of the Scriptural hope
of Israel, of a Redeemer who was to "come

Jacob." To my surprise, he told me that he
believed all that had been prophesied of in the
Scriptures had been fulfilled in Christianity.
I asked if he then believed Jesus to be the
Messiah of the Jews. To this he evaded

giving a direct answer; but seemed to regard Him in the light of a reformer of morals, and to view Christianity as the instrument of civilising the human race; of which civilisation all may enjoy the benefit, whatever his own private religious opinions are. He did not believe any change of religion necessary. "I am born a Jew, and shall die a Jew." I spoke to him of the fallen state of man, and pressed on him the subjects of death, judgment, and eternity, in which there is no support for the mind of man, save in a Mediator. But all this was as "idle tales" to him; he had no solid belief in a future state; there may be and there may not be; we cannot tell anything about it.

This is perhaps the most hopeless state of mind for the reception of Divine truth. The weeds of superstition may be rooted out, and the good seed sown in their room; but in the barren soil of infidelity, nothing of a spiritual kind can grow. Yet are we not, on that account, to withhold the presentation of truth; the Holy Spirit can take of the things of Christ, and effectually show them, even to the most hardened infidel; changing the barren soil into a fruitful field.

I found many Jews on the continent, especially in France, who had read the New Testament, which the London Jews' Society have
largely distributed. This is a great step
gained, as the word of truth may be brought
home to their conscience in a time and manner
they little expect.

The Jews in the south of Europe have less
acquaintance with Christianity than the Jews
of France and Germany; but even among
them there appears some shaking of the dry
bones. Amongst the younger members of the
community there seems a growing discontent
with their present position; a desire for reform
of some kind, some better religious standing,
that is yet short of apostacy from Judaism.
Among such, an able and judicious missionary,
may find many openings.

The Jews, who are natives of the East, are
like the other inhabitants, less intelligent than
the Europeans. Indeed, as may naturally be
expected, the character of the Jew in every
country, is considerably modified by that of
the people among whom he dwells. A great
proportion of the Jews in Syria, however, are

not natives of the East, but Europeans who, from various motives, settle there. From my interviews with them I shall select such particulars as may be interesting.

I found many of them very devout, but at the same time bigoted and superstitious. They are generally great students of the Talmud. In one of the towns I met an interesting young Jew lately arrived from Russia, who had accompanied his father to settle in the Holy Land. He expressed himself not satisfied with the measure of learning among the Jews in the town where his father had fixed his abode. I asked him if he considered himself a competent judge of his brethren's learning : he said he was ; and mentioned as a proof of this, that he knew several volumes of the Talmud by heart. I asked if he knew much of the Bible by heart. He said : "No, it is not the fashion among us to learn the Bible by heart." I asked him why his father had left Russia to settle in Palestine? He said it was on account of the superior piety of the Jews in the latter country. "The prayers here are most excellent," said he : meaning, of course, that they are uttered in a devotional spirit, since the liturgy is alike everywhere. I inquired as to his views about the coming of the Messiah. He said: "We must expect his coming every day, but still he will not come till he pleases." He had no doubt the Messiah will come and establish his kingdom; and that this will probably take place at the end of the six thousand years from the creation.

One old man asked me: What good have people derived from their belief in Jesus of Nazareth? This question I endeavoured to answer by explaining the nature and effects of Christianity. "If this were the case," said he, "we should find Christians the best people in the world instead of the worst. The Mohammedans are not nearly so bad as the Christians; they do not oppress us so much."

to persuade him that the Eastern Christians are no Christians at all. I fear my readers will be weary of the constant recurrence of this subject; my apology is, that it met me at every turn; that never did I converse with a Jew who did not bring it forward; that it is, in fact, the greatest of all outward obstacles in the way of any really pious and respectable Jew giving the subject of Christianity a moment's consideration.

I read to the old man our Lord's sermon on the mount, as having been the first passage in the New Testament that particularly impressed me. He listened with great attention, and said: "If these principles were carried out, the world would be in a very different state from what it is at present." Before we parted he gave me a solemn admonition on the sin of forsaking the religion of my fathers; and asked what benefit I had received that could compensate for being cut off from the people of God. This gave me a farther opportunity of explaining to him the unsearchable riches of Christ. Among other things I had gained, I could assure him that I possessed a much more intense love of my brethren than ever I had before I was a Christian.

In conversing with another aged Jew on the subject of a new birth unto righteousness, I was forcibly reminded of Nicodemus. "What!" said he, with a smile, "must I be born again?

I am an old man, must I become a little infant again ?" The things of the Spirit of God must always appear foolishness to the natural man.

I think that in tracts written for distribution among the Jews, the fall of man, and couse-quent depravity of human nature ought to be brought prominently forward. There is in every man's conscience a feeling that, to a certain extent, responds to the truth of this, and it is the foundation of all Christian doctrine; it is that which renders a mediator between God and man needful. It is also desirable to point out to them, that in Scripture the judg-ments of God are not denounced against them for the neglect of outward worship, but for the alienation of their hearts from God, and to appeal to them as to whether that alienation does not continue still. And they should be reminded, that a restoration to their own land, with the addition of all outward prosperity, could not make them happy, unless they expe-rienced a moral and spiritual renovation; unless they received the "new heart and new spirit" promised by God.

I must now, according to the request of many friends, give my views as to the best mode of endeavouring to convert my brethren to Christianity. It is asked by some : Why have any particular mode of converting Jews? May they not be converted, like any other sinners, simply by the preaching of the Gospel? Most certainly they might, if we could only get them to come to hear it. If the Jews would regularly attend the ministrations of a faithful preacher of the Gospel, nothing more would be required. But before they can be brought to do this, much previous persuasion and instruction is required. No Jew would regularly attend a Christian place of worship, until he had made up his mind to abandon Judaism. In the first age of Christianity, the great majority of them were converted in their own land by their own brethren; those scattered in the Roman provinces, were preached to in their own synagogues. Although Christianity and the human heart remain unaltered, man's outward circumstances are changed from age to age; and the outward means we use for bringing the truths of the Gospel to bear upon

the mind of man, must be in some measure
altered to suit these outward circumstances.
The first evangelists preached to the crowd in
the open air; this plan has in all ages, down
to the present day, been pursued, and often
successfully; but when attempted a few years
back* with the Jews, there was nothing but
scenes of riot and confusion. People are apt
to forget that the Gospel of Christ has to en-
counter from the Jews, not merely the natural
enmity of the carnal mind, but the prejudice
against Christianity caused by more than a
thousand years of bitter persecution from nominal Christians, and by the vice and ungodliness
they daily behold among them. In short, the
difficulties and obstacles in the way of a Jew's
conversion, can only be fully known to those
who labour among them. In stating what I
conceive to be the most eligible mode of
attempting a mission among the Jews, let it
not be said that I look too much to human
instrumentality. I am quite convinced that
God could bless any instrument, or that He

* By the Rev. Edward Irving.

could convert the whole world, if He pleased,

has not only commanded human efforts, but in His providential dealings with men, we do not find that He ordinarily works with instruments that are in themselves inefficient. No one can deny that He might, had He so pleased, have brought about the Reformation by an ignorant peasant; but He chose to do it by a Luther.

I have no hesitation in saying, that the first thing requisite in establishing a mission to the Jews, is to find out a man fit for the work. A man may have piety, and zeal, and learning, and yet be utterly unfit for it. Unless his piety be combined with an ardent love to the Jews as the chosen people of God, he is quite unfit to be a missionary to them. Unless his zeal be guided by a knowledge of the Jewish charac- ter, its habits, its prejudices, its peculiar tem- perament, it will then be a zeal not "according to knowledge." And unless his learning con- sist of that which the Jews account learning, it is to them no learning at all. They have as little understanding of, and as little respect for, that which constitutes the glory of a senior wrangler or first-class man, as the man of Oxford or Cambridge has for the learning of the Talmud. A missionary to the Jews must be able to meet them on their own ground ; must not only have patience to listen to their questions and cavils, but ability to answer them. Many things that may appear mere captious objections to a Gentile Christian, are really difficulties that occur to the Jewish mind ; warped as it is, in some points, by early associations.

It is very awkward to speak of living characters, (and yet long may the one of whom I am now to speak continue to present this obstacle to freedom of animadversion,) but the case of the Rev. Dr. Duncan at Pesth, so completely answers my idea of what a mission to the Jews ought to be, that I must be permitted to adduce it. Here is a man who is learned, not only in a Gentile, but in a Jewish sense ; and one, whose age and position in society, show the Jews at once that he is not a mere hireling ; but that, on the contrary, for such a man to become a missionary to the Jews, is a positive sacrifice in a worldly point

of view.   It surely will not be supposed that I
mean to say a young missionary may not be
equally sincere and self-denying; but to the
Jews this is not so obvious; in very many
cases they settle the whole matter satisfactorily
to their own minds, by saying, "He is paid
for it."

Dr. Duncan settled down quietly among the
Jews at Pesth, opening his house to them,
conciliating them by kindness; conversing, ar-
guing, reading with them; admitting them to
the hospitalities of a well-ordered family.   For
more than a year nothing seemed to have been
done; but there was an under current at work
that in due time was made manifest; and it
has resulted in decidedly the most successful
work among the Jews of modern times.   Their
Rabbis cannot affect to despise a man of his
undoubted learning: nor can the Jews in their
hearts believe that he is actuated by any thing
but love to their nation.   Some, it is true,
have resorted to the old cry that has been
raised against faithful missionaries in all ages,
that his efforts are connected with political
movements; but happily he, and the brethren

who are now there, have no difficulty in disproving such a charge.

But to all this it may be objected, that we cannot meet every day with such men as Dr. Duncan and Dr. M'Caul. To this I can only reply, that in the present state of awakened feeling about the Jews, we may hope that men of piety and talent will use the same means to fit themselves for the work that these have done, and may be as willing to devote their energies to the cause of Israel. But it is chiefly at the commencement of a mission that such men are needed. When the work is once begun, labourers of a more ordinary kind may carry it on, though of course it is desirable that their attainments should never fall much below this standard.

I must also express my strong conviction of the importance of London as a station for a mission to the Jews. There are more than twice as many Jews in London as in the whole of Palestine, while the number of actual labourers among them is small indeed, compared with those in Palestine. In Beyrout there are but twenty-four Jewish families; and when I

was there this scanty population had two missionaries! A really efficient mission in London,
so managed as to bring forward young men of
intelligence and education, might be a nursery
for missionaries to the Jews in every part of
the world.   Like Jerusalem on the day of Pen-
tecost, there are dwelling in London Jews "out
of every nation under heaven;" and in no other
place are there such facilities for gaining acquaintance with all that a missionary ought to
know. My full conviction is, that London
ought to be regarded as the principal mis
sionary station, and that any decided movement
among the Jews in London would attract more
general notice than a movement in any other
part of the world.

I must now say a few words on a subject
that is frequently discussed at present,—the
propriety of giving temporal relief in connexion with the religious instruction of the Jews.
No doubt it may be given, and probably is
often given, in such an injudicious way as to
operate as a bounty upon hypocrisy. The best
way to avoid this is, where cases of real distress are presented, let them be relieved simply

on the score of benevolence ; since if they can meet with sympathy and relief as poor Jews, there will be no need to pretend a desire to inquire into Christianity.

After many years experience, I have come, I may say almost against my will, to the conclusion, that little can be done in this country towards the conversion of the Jews without a temporary home for the shelter of inquirers. Indeed this, with the necessary expense attending it, seems to me one of the chief reasons for carrying on measures for the conversion of Jews in this country by means of a public society. On the continent matters are very different. Suppose a Jew in any rank of life to be awakened there, it may happen that there is not within his reach any really pious minister who may hold forth to him the word of life. A missionary to the Jews is, therefore, indispensable. But in England if any Jew, not merely in the upper ranks of society, but any tradesman or journeyman who is able to support himself by his daily labour, wishes to inquire into the truth of Christianity, he will never think of going to a society for this pur-

pose; he will apply for instruction to some
minister of the gospel, or Christian friend.
For these, therefore, no special missionary nor
society is needed; in the privacy of their own
house or lodging they may search the Scriptures, unmolested by Rabbi or Elder of the
synagogue.

Very different is the case of the poor wan-
derer, who earns his livelihood by going from
town to town; whose home is a public-house;
whose daily companions are the dregs of society." Why," perhaps some committee-man
of a Jews' society may say, "Why cannot
the Jews learn religion like other people?
Let them read the Scriptures diligently,
and come to our missionaries with their
difficulties. All this they may do without
forsaking their lawful callings, and throwing
themselves on us for maintenance." Ah!
friend, wouldst thou reason thus if that poor
Jew were thine own prodigal son? Wouldst
thou say: "My son, it is true, is not in the
best possible circumstances for attending to the
concerns of his soul. He travels with jewellery;
finds his best customers among the wretched

inhabitants of the haunts of infamy; constantly associates with the worst of characters;
spends his evenings in the tavern, and throws
himself down to sleep in one corner of a room
occupied by several others. Nevertheless, if
he is sincere, there is nothing in all this to
hinder him to become a Christian." Is he
to take out his Bible, and diligently study
it, amid the sounds of the fiddle and the
drunken song? Is he to kneel down and
pray amid the shouts of derision, the filthy
and blasphemous jests of the wretched crew
around him? Even in this state, doubtless,
the grace of God could reach his heart; but
this mode of reasoning would set aside all
efforts of a spiritual kind whatsoever; ministers, missionaries, churches, and private
Christians, might desist from seeking the conversion of sinners; might comfortably fold
their hands and go to sleep, justifying themselves by the orthodox doctrine, that God can
do it all very well without them!

" But then," says the objector, " if we had
a home, however homely, it would hold out an
inducement to persons to pretend to be in-

quirers into Christianity, for the sake of board
and lodging." No doubt it might; and therefore a sound discretion must be exercised in
the admission of inmates, who ought at first
to be received only for a month on probation,
during which time a superintendent of ordinary
discernment would be in a great measure able
to judge of their sincerity. The outlay of some
forty shillings would not be so great an evil,
to rescue a poor Jew for a whole month from
the polluting influence of evil association, and to
place him in the genial atmosphere of Christian
kindness and purity; to instruct him in the word
of God; to warn, to exhort, and to encourage
him to cast himself as a helpless sinner on the
free mercy of God in Christ Jesus. Suppose we
give the largest allowance of such hypocrites
for which any objector would contend; suppose there should be one every month; then,
at an outlay of one pound in every thousand
of the annual income of the London Jews'
Society, we should have twelve Jews furnished
with such knowledge as might, though now
rejected, afterwards become to them "a savour
of life unto life." If to any of them it should

become " a savour of death unto death," his blood will be upon his own head, and will not be required at the hands of the society.*

At first sight, it appears desirable to combine manual labour with religious instruction, as in the Operative Jewish Institution in London. But the great expense incurred in teaching, and carrying on any branch of trade, is not compensated by equivalent benefit to the inmates. Men in such circumstances do not learn a trade thoroughly enough to be able afterwards to gain a livelihood by it. In cases where it is considered desirable that a person should learn a mechanical trade, it would be much better, after he has been instructed in Christianity, to apprentice him to a pious tradesman.

In regard to what may be called the aggressive measures of a Jews' society, the mode in which they should seek to excite a spirit of inquiry amongst Jews, I do not think any

* In Liverpool, an institution such as I have described, supported and managed by members of the Church of England, has been carried on for some years with great success.

rules that may be laid down are of much value. I can only repeat, get fit men, and when they are fairly engaged in the work they will find fit measures. Lectures, tracts, visits,—all are good, if well managed; all are worthless if not well managed. Some well-meaning men may spend their lives in talking on religion to Jews, with no other result than that of greatly encreasing the difficulties of those who come after them on a like errand.

The separate and scattered state of believing Jews is much to be regretted. Many of them, especially in the higher classes of society, become completely amalgamated with their Gentile brethren, and cease to be known as Jews at all, while the great majority are driven hither and thither, by the difficulty of obtaining " the meat which perisheth." Nothing would tend so much to excite a spirit of inquiry amongst the Jews as the movements of a body of their converted brethren; not as forming themselves into a new sect in the Christian church, but as bearing a united testimony for Christ before their brethren : co-operating with heart and hand for the spiritual and temporal good of Israel. I conclude by affectionately urging the consideration of this on all my converted brethren, reminding them, that in becoming Christians, they do not cease to be Jews, and that, "for their brethren and companions' sakes," they ought still to bear, if it yet be so, the reproach of belonging to that despised race; despised by men, but beloved by God for the fathers' sakes.

Printed by J. Unwin, 31, Bucklersbury, London.

DOCTRINES

OF

THE GREEK CHURCH.

The following account of the Greek Church is written by a gentleman who has resided many years in the East. It may serve to correct the vague ideas entertained of it in this country, and dispel the notion of its being greatly superior to the Romish Church in purity of doctrine, which generally obtains among those who are little acquainted with it.

The Rev. H. Southgate, delegate of the American Protestant Episcopal Church at Constantinople, has declared,* "The more I see of the Eastern Churches, the more deeply I am convinced that a union between them and us is practicable without

* See letter of Mr. S. to Mr. Tomlinson, Secretary of the Society for Promoting Christian Knowledge.

AA

any sacrifice of Catholic principle." And again,* "So far as my own knowledge yet goes, I can perceive nothing in the Eastern Churches to which I could make exception, if their whole form of worship and rites were imbued with a spiritual life. The want of this, and not false doctrines (as purgatory and transubstantiation; nor practices in themselves unchristian, as worshipping the host in the Romish Church), is the grand and sole corruption, so far as I yet know." Mr. Southgate's attention was called to this latter extract by certain clergymen in his own Church, at a subsequent period, but while he replied to some other strictures of theirs, he takes no notice of this paragraph, so that it may fairly be presumed that his views of the Eastern Churches remain unchanged. The same ideas of the practicability of a union with the Eastern Churches *without any sacrifice of*

to the Eastern ecclesiastics, recommendatory of Bishop Alexander, by the Archbishop of Canterbury, that that prelate and his advisers hold similar sentiments.

Mr. Southgate sees nothing amiss in the Eastern Churches, if only the whole form of worship and

imbued with spiritual life means, I suppose, when

* See *Spirit of Missions*, of Feb., 1841, an American Episcopal Church periodical.

we speak of acts of religious worship, that the Holy Spirit is present with the worshipper, accompanying or inditing his prayers, and giving life and power to the word heard or read. We are taught in the Scriptures, that in acceptable prayer the spirit maketh intercession for us, and we are said to be sanctified through the truth. (Rom. viii. 26 ; John xvii. 17.) Now, if God be the only proper object of prayer, can we expect him to give his Spirit in aid of petitions addressed to false gods or to angels, or to departed saints? Take, for instance, the following prayer, used in the Syrian Greek Church, as well as in the Maronite Chapel : "O Virgin, mother of God, forsake me not who am seeking from thee victory and help. Have mercy on me, for in thee do I place my trust. O thou who art free from fault, grant me fountains of tears, that in them I may wash away my many sins, for in thee do I place all my hope. O, the espoused of God, hasten to my succour and deliverance before I perish, that I may escape from the hands of malicious devices, and from the last awful catastrophe." Now, what say we to this? Can such a prayer be imbued with spiritual life? In other words, can we believe that such petitions, thus addressed, are ever indited or accompanied by the Holy Spirit? I tremble as I copy this prayer, and remember the High and Holy One who has declared, " My glory will I not give to another, neither my praise to graven images." And I tremble yet more when I hear a professedly Protestant missionary say, the forms are good,—they *only need to be imbued with spiritual life.* Perhaps Mr. S. will say he never saw this prayer, as it seems to be used in Syria, and so feels himself acquitted. But if not this, he must have examined very superficially not to have found others equally blasphemous. He reads Greek I believe; let him run over the service books of the "Orthodox Eastern Church," and the authorized expositions of them, and he will decide, if he be truly a Protestant, that something more is needed than that the existing forms be imbued with a spiritual life. Let him examine, for instance, the little manual called the *Synopsis*, and he will find therein nine prayers addressed to the Virgin Mary, one of them twelve pages in length. In these prayers he will hear her called "our shield," "our hope," "our only refuge," "*our propitiation;*" he will hear her addressed in language such as should be used only in approaching the Supreme Being; and blessings asked such as he alone can grant. Mr. Southgate's language certainly implies that he has not been inattentive to the dogmas and practices of the Eastern Churches. How, then, he could hazard such un-Protestant assertions must be left for himself to explain.

In the religious systems of the East, the Church is really put in the place of Christ, tradition in the place or alongside of the Scriptures, and the altar in the place of the pulpit. The people are taught to speak of union with the Church very much as

Protestants are accustomed to speak of union with
Christ: instead of " out of me ye can do nothing,"
it is, "out of the Church ye can do nothing."
The Church feeds, teaches, saves. And by Church
is not meant the invisible *Church,* out of which
we all confess, there is no salvation, but this or
that organization, of necessity Episcopal; some-
limiting the possibility of salvation to their own
communion, and others very considerately extend-
ing it. " The Church," says an old Greek* writer,
and a sanctioned expositor of the Liturgy, "*is
married to Christ through baptism and unction
and ordination and the communion, and the other
mysteries ;*" not a word being said about faith.
And the authorized expounders of the Canons (see
Πηδάλιον, page thirty one, Athen's edition) say,
that the grace of the Holy Spirit no longer resides
in the Romish Church, *because trine immersion is
not practised there.* In this scheme salvation is
made to depend entirely upon the performance of
certain *ceremonies,* and these ceremonies performed
in a particular way.

This invisible, intangible corporation called the
Church, is supposed to be pervaded in all its offices
and ordinances with the Holy Spirit, however

* Simon, Archbishop of Thessalonica, in the fifteenth
century. His works have been translated into modern
Greek, and published with a recommendation by one of
the patriarchs. Jeremiah, Patriarch of Constantinople,
in his discussion with the German Divines, in the sixteenth century, made constant use of his writings.

wicked the officers may be, and however absurd
and unscriptural the ordinances. To this corporation the spirit is supposed to be limited in all his
gracious influences. The expounders of the Greek
Canons, as we have just seen, expressly attest that
the Spirit does not reside in the Romish Church,
principally because trine immersion is not practised there; and of course he cannot dwell in any
of the Protestant Churches. The Spirit is conveyed only through certain channels, and its
conveyance depends upon the will of certain men;
" for," say the expounders alluded to, " it is by
the grace of the Holy Spirit that the orthodox
(i. e. the Greek) priests perform the mysteries.
All others being unbaptized, have not that grace,
and of course cannot transmit it." What follows?
An individual not within the precincts of this
imaginary corporation cannot receive the Holy
Spirit. He must be transferred *within* those limits.
But how is the transfer accomplished? Only by
baptism. Here, then, we have the origin of the
doctrine of *baptismal regeneration.* Without trine
immersion, a man cannot get within the boundaries
of the operation of Divine grace. With it he
comes into a territory, every part of which is full
of the Spirit. Even the water and the oil and the
bread in that blissful region are redolent of grace,
and the hands that administer them are all holy.

Mr. Southgate sees nothing in the Eastern
Churches as incompatible with a union, without
any sacrifice of Catholic principle. All that is

necessary is, that the existing forms of worship and rites be imbued with a spiritual life. Let us, then, look a little more in detail at some of these rites, as practised among the Greeks. I shall again quote from the Archbishop of Thessalonica, whose exposition of the *service books* is so highly esteemed among the ecclesiastics. In his explanation of the baptismal service, we have these words—" After a little delay, the priest breathes upon the water three times, thus infusing it with the more richly Divine grace in imitation of Christ, and in accordance with the word which says, the Lord moved upon the water, and which had reference to baptism. He then again seals the water with his hands, making the sign of the cross, and saying, " Let all opposing powers within be destroyed, that the water may become spiritual and holy, that no evil of the devil may be concealed in it, and that it may be able to create anew, to sanctify and to change into the sons of God such as are baptized in the same, and make them the children of light." After a description of certain other ceremonies preparatory to the baptism, he adds, " Then the laver is filled with the Holy Ghost, and the water contains within itself the invisible Christ." After the baptism we have this paragraph : " The Divine water of baptism in which sin has been drowned, and into which Christ and the Holy Spirit have come, and wherein the man has been renewed, should be poured out in some sacred place, and not where the feet of those who do not understand

this mystery can tread upon it." Once more from
the same author: "When the baptized person has
been regenerated (baptized), he comes out new and
enlightened, and the son of God, from the holy
laver, our spiritual mother, which is in place of
the pure and holy womb of the mother of God."
" As the pure blood and holy womb of the virgin,
through means of the Holy Ghost, effected the
incarnation of the Word of God, so the pure water
of the laver and the Holy Ghost (*i. e.* the Spirit
in the water as in the womb of the virgin) have
wrought our pure second birth." Let any one
carefully read the prayers and exorcisms, as used
in the baptismal service, and he will see that, awful
as the preceding language of the Archbishop is,
he is a devout and faithful expositor. Now, what
says Mr. S. to this? Will there be no sacrifice of
principle in effecting a union with a, Church that
holds such views? Is *this* form very good, and
does it only need to be imbued with a spiritual life
to make it acceptable to a Protestant clergyman?

Let us turn now to the *Communion Service.*
And here we have for our teacher one of the patriarchs of Constantinople, Jeremiah, who lived in
the latter part of the sixteenth century. About
thirty years after Luther's death, several learned
German divines, one of them a professor in the
University of Tubingen, opened a correspondence
with the Patriarch just mentioned, on the subject
of the differences between the Protestants and
Romanists. The divines had hoped to find that

the dogmas of the Greek Church were substantially accordant with their Protestant views. The reply of the Patriarch, in three long letters, in which he exhibits in detail the doctrines of that Church, dispelled all their hopes. They had sent him the *Confession of Augsburg*, and had in a masterly manner answered two of his letters. But in his final reply, the Patriarch tells them that while they rejected some of the Sacraments, they perverted those they did receive ; and he closes by begging them to write no more on theological subjects, inasmuch as they were determined to wrest from him the authority in which be trusted, viz., the holy and divine words of the Fathers.

The Patriarch says, in regard to the *Communion*, "The bread becomes the body of Christ, and the wine and water becomes the blood of Christ by the intervention of the Holy Ghost, who changes them in a way incomprehensible to the reason and understanding of man. The bread, I say, and the wine and water are changed by the Holy Spirit, in an incomprehensible manner, and are no longer two, but one and the same. The bread and wine are not the symbols of the body and blood of Christ (God forbid), but the very deified body of the Lord." Page 184, "*The Catholic Church* (i. e. the Greek) *has determined* that after the consecration the bread is changed into the very body of Christ, and the wine into the very blood of Christ, by the Holy Spirit." Page 49, " By the grace of the Almighty Spirit the bread is changed and converted into the very body of the Lord, and the wine into the very blood of the Lord."

Here, then, we have the doctrine of transubstantiation expressed in words the most explicit. And does this constitute no obstacle to the so much talked of union?

The principal repository of Divine grace in this Church system is the *chrism,* or *anointing oil;* into the baptismal water, grace is conveyed as occasion demands; but in the chrism it has a permanent abode. For the Greek Church it is prepared at Constantinople by the Patriarch and his clergy. A long service is read over it, and a multitude of prayers offered; and during the process, the Holy Spirit is supposed to descend and diffuse himself through it. It is thence sent to the various churches, as need requires, and kept most reverentially; the people generally seeming to have no other idea of the Divine Spirit than as contained in this oil. For the Armenians it is made at Echmiadzin, the seat of their Patriarch, and in the several churches it is kept in small vessels, made in the form of a dove, which, I have been told by Armenians, the people actually call the Holy Spirit. "By this chrism," says the expounder of the Liturgy, whom we have before quoted, "Christ is formed in our hearts, and we become the temple of God the Father, and also of his Son Jesus Christ, and of the Holy Spirit. This chrism, therefore, completes our baptism, and makes us temples of the Trinity. On this account it is used after baptism, and gives us the indwelling of the Spirit."

Does Mr. S. see nothing *here* in the way of a union with the Eastern Churches?

Mr. S. tells us, in an extract at the beginning of this article, that he discovers as yet in the " Eastern Churches " no " false doctrines," " nor practices in themselves unchristian." We leave it for our readers to decide, if *they* do not find both, from the quotations we have made from the highest authorities in the Greek Church. On this subject we shall not enter at present, if at all. A volume, rather than an essay, would be required to do justice to it. C.

P.S.—We have alluded to a Greek manual of prayer, called the *Synopsis*, and to the fact that it contains nine prayers, one of them twelve pages in length, to the Virgin Mary. We add here a short extract from another of them : "Thou knowest, O mistress, mother of God, that I am as a foreign bird, not knowing where to lay my head, except on the mother of Christ and our God. Thou, O mistress, art my help, *thou my propitiation*, thou my shield, *thou my sponsor before God*, thou my father, thou my mother, thou my guide. In thee I repose all my hope," &c. &c.

WS - #0178 - 281024 - C0 - 229/152/15 - PB - 9781331314363 - Gloss Lamination